Who's Driving

Jack Stilgoe

Who's Driving Innovation?

New Technologies and the Collaborative State

Jack Stilgoe
Department of Science
and Technology Studies
University College London
London, UK

ISBN 978-3-030-32319-6   ISBN 978-3-030-32320-2   (eBook)
https://doi.org/10.1007/978-3-030-32320-2

This Palgrave Macmillan imprint is published by the registered company Springer Nature
Switzerland AG
The registered company address is: Gewerbestrasse 11, 6330 Cham, Switzerland

ACKNOWLEDGEMENTS

The ideas that led to this book began to form during a summer at the Centre for the Study of the Sciences and the Humanities in Bergen. Thank you to Matthias Kaiser and his colleagues for having me to stay. Research for the book has been supported by the Alan Turing Institute, the European Commission, as part of the SCALINGS project (Horizon 2020 grant 788359), and the Economic and Social Research Council, who fund the *Driverless Futures?* project (grant ES/S001832/1). I was lucky to have conversations and comments on drafts from a number of experts, including Jamie Bartlett, Peter Bradwell, Tom Cohen, Diane Coyle, Stanley Flink, Milos Mladenovic, Saba Mirza, Melanie Smallman, Langdon Winner and three anonymous reviewers. Finally, thanks are due to my colleagues and students at University College London's Department of Science and Technology Studies.

CONTENTS

CONTENTS

CHAPTER 1

Who Killed Elaine Herzberg?

Elaine Herzberg did not know that she was part of an experiment. She was walking her bicycle across the road at 10 p.m. on a dark desert night in Tempe, Arizona. Having crossed three lanes of a four-lane highway, Herzberg was run down by a Volvo SUV travelling at 38 miles per hour. She was pronounced dead at 10:30 p.m.

The next day, the officer in charge of the investigation rushed to blame the pedestrian. Police Chief Sylvia Moir told a local newspaper, 'It's very clear it would have been difficult to avoid this collision... she came from the shadows right into the roadway... the driver said it was like a flash.'[1] According to the rules of the road, Herzberg should not have been there. Had she been at the crosswalk just down the road, things would probably have turned out differently.

Rafaela Vasquez was behind the wheel of the Volvo, but she wasn't driving. The car, operated by Uber, was in 'autonomous' mode. Vasquez's job was to monitor the computer that was doing the driving and take over if anything went wrong. A few days after the crash, the police released a video from a camera on the rear-view mirror. It showed Vasquez looking down at her knees in the seconds before the crash and for almost a third of the 21-minute journey that led up to it. Data taken from her phone suggested that she had been watching an episode of 'The Voice' rather than the road. Embarrassingly for the police chief, her colleagues' investigation calculated that, had Vasquez been looking at the road, she would have seen Herzberg and been able to stop more than 40 feet before impact.[2]

© The Author(s) 2020
J. Stilgoe, *Who's Driving Innovation?*,
https://doi.org/10.1007/978-3-030-32320-2_1

1

Drivers and pedestrians make mistakes all the time. A regularly repeated statistic is that more than 90% of crashes are caused by human error. The Tempe Police report concluded that the crash had been caused by human frailties on both sides: Herzberg should not have been in the road; Vasquez for her part should have seen the pedestrian, she should have taken control of the car and she should have been paying attention to her job. In the crash investigation business, these factors are known as 'proximate causes'. But if we focus only on proximate causes, we fail to learn from the novelty of the situation. Herzberg was the first pedestrian to be killed by a self-driving car. The Uber crash was not just a case of human error. It was also a failure of technology.

Here was a car on a public road in which the driving had been delegated to a computer. A thing that had very recently seemed impossible had become, on the streets of Arizona, mundane—so mundane that the person who was supposed to be monitoring the system had, in effect, switched off.[3] The car's sensors—360-degree radar, short- and long-range cameras, a lidar laser scanner on the roof and a GPS system—were supposed to provide superhuman awareness of the surroundings. The car's software was designed to interpret this information based on thousands of hours of similar experiences, identifying objects, predicting what they were going to do next and plotting a safe route. This was artificial intelligence in the wild: not playing chess or translating text but steering two tonnes of metal.

When high-profile transport disasters happen in the US, the National Transportation Safety Board is called in. The NTSB are less interested in blame than in learning from mistakes to make things safer. Their investigations are part of the reason why air travel is so astonishingly safe. In 2017, for the first time, a whole year passed in which not a single person died in a commercial passenger jet crash. If self-driving cars are going to be as safe as aeroplanes, regulators need to listen to the NTSB. The Board's report on the Uber crash concluded that the car's sensors had detected an object in the road six seconds before the crash, but the software 'did not include a consideration for jaywalking pedestrians'.[4] The AI could not work out what Herzberg was and the car continued on its path. A second before the car hit Herzberg, the driver took the wheel but swerved only slightly. Vasquez only applied the brakes after the crash.

In addition to the proximate causes, Elaine Herzberg's death was the result of a set of more distant choices about technology and how it should be developed. Claiming that they were in a race against other manufacturers, Uber chose to test their system quickly and cheaply. Other self-driving car companies put two or more qualified engineers in each of their test vehicles. Vasquez was alone and she was no test pilot. The only qualification she needed before starting work was a driving licence.

Uber's strategy filtered all the way down into its cars' software, which was much less intelligent than the company's hype had implied. As the company's engineers worked out how to make sense of the information coming from the car's sensors, they balanced the risk of a false positive (detecting a thing that isn't really there) against the risk of a false negative (failing to react to an object that turns out to be dangerous). After earlier tests of self-driving cars in which software overreacted to things like steam, plastic bags and shadows on the roads, engineers retuned their systems. The misidentification of Elaine Herzberg was partly the result of a conscious choice about how safe the technology needed to be in order to be safe enough. One engineer at Uber later told a journalist that the company had 'refused to take responsibility. They blamed it on the homeless lady [Herzberg], the Latina with a criminal record driving the car [Vasquez], even though we all knew Perception [Uber's software] was broken.'⁵

The companies that had built the hardware also blamed Uber. The president of Velodyne, the manufacturer of the car's main sensors, told Bloomberg, 'Certainly, our lidar is capable of clearly imaging Elaine and her bicycle in this situation. However, our lidar doesn't make the decision to put on the brakes or get out of her way.'⁶ Volvo made clear that they had nothing to do with the experiment. They provided the body of the car, not its brain. An automatic braking system that was built into the Volvo—using well-established technology—would almost certainly have saved Herzberg's life, but this had been switched off by Uber engineers, who were testing their own technology and didn't want interference from another system.

We don't know what Elaine Herzberg was thinking when she set off across the road. Nor do we know exactly what the car was thinking. Machines make decisions differently from humans and the decisions made by machine learning systems are often inscrutable. However, the evidence from the crash points to a reckless approach to the development of a new technology. Uber shouldered some of the blame, agreeing an out-of-court settlement with the victim's family and changing their approach to safety. But to point the finger only at the company would be to ignore the context. Roads are dangerous places, particularly in the US and particularly for pedestrians. A century of decisions by policymakers and carmakers has produced a system that gives power and freedom to drivers. Tempe, part of the sprawling metropolitan area of Phoenix, is car-friendly. The roads are wide and neat and the weather is good. It is ideally suited to testing a self-driving car. For a pedestrian, the place and its infrastructure can feel hostile. Official statistics bear this out. In 2017, Arizona was the most dangerous state for pedestrians in the US.[7]

Members of Herzberg's family sued the state government on the grounds that, first, the streets were unsafe for pedestrians and, second, policymakers were complicit in Uber's experiments. In addition to the climate and the tidiness of the roads, Uber had been attracted to Tempe by the governor of Arizona, Doug Ducey. The company had started their testing in San Francisco, near their headquarters. But when one of their self-driving cars ran a red light, California regulators told Uber that they needed a $150 permit. Uber objected and Ducey seized his opportunity. With the Governor's blessing, the company had already been testing in secret on the streets of Phoenix. Ducey could now go public and claim that he had tempted a big tech company away from Silicon Valley. He tweeted 'This is what over-regulation looks like #ditchcalifornia' and 'Here in AZ we WELCOME this kind of technology & innovation! #ditchcalifornia #AZmeansBIZ'. With almost no oversight, Uber moved their experiments to Arizona in 2016. When Herzberg was killed less than 18 months later, Ducey's enthusiasm collapsed and Uber were thrown out of their new laboratory.

When technologies fail, it is often hard to find the person responsible and easy for those involved to blame others or claim it was a freak occurrence. It's a symptom of a wider problem, which is that we aren't clear who is in control of the development of new technologies. When technological dreams meet the real world, the results are often disappointing and occasionally messy. Policymakers are seduced by the promise of new technologies, which arrive without instructions for how they should be governed. It is all too common for regulation to be an afterthought. In the world of aviation, it's called a tombstone mentality: defects are noticed, lessons are learned and rules are written in grim hindsight. In Arizona, policymakers allowed a private experiment to take place in public, with citizens as unwitting participants. It ended badly for everyone involved. Tragedies are opportunities for learning, opportunities to challenge claims made about technology and opportunities to think about alternatives. We should ask if a technology is safe enough, but this also means asking, Safe enough for what? Why are self-driving cars being developed? Where are they taking us? As politicians compete in their enthusiasm for innovation, such questions often go unasked. Two months after the crash, the Governor of Ohio announced plans to make his state 'the wild, wild West' for unregulated self-driving car testing.[8]

It is vital to scrutinise technologies at an early stage, before they become just another fact of life. If we agree that technology is too important to be left to technology companies, we are left with the challenge of how to democratise innovation. New technologies should prompt us to update the question posed by political scientist Robert Dahl (1961): 'Who governs?'[9] If we are to hang on to democracy in the twenty-first century, we should keep asking 'Who's driving?'

The hope that powers this book is that we can do better and imagine a proactive role for policymakers and citizens. I want to make the case that new technologies can and should be redirected towards public benefit. In the next chapter, I ask why we fall into the trap of thinking that technologies are autonomous and inevitable. Chapter 3 is about the politics of innovation: who benefits and who decides? Chapter 4 focuses on hype, which is used by technology developers as a way to stake claims on the future. The final chapter is an argument for collaboration between the developers of technology, governments and citizens. The book uses self-driving cars as an example, but its messages are relevant to other new technologies, particularly those in the area of artificial intelligence, whose rules have not yet been written and whose destinies have not yet been set. If our technological future is to incorporate democratic values, policymakers will need to challenge the story of technological inevitability, resist hype, target the needs of those who often lose out from innovation and enable new collaborations to flourish.

NOTES

1. Tempe police chief says early probe shows no fault by Uber, San Francisco Chronicle, 26 March 2018, https://www.sfchronicle.com/business/article/ Exclusive-Tempe-police-chief-says-early-probe-12765481.php.
2. Tempe police department general offense report, March 2018.
3. Research with autopilots in aircraft has revealed the detrimental effects of automation on people's concentration in the short term and skills in the long term. The idea of the human-on-the-loop, overseeing an automated system, looks near-fatally flawed. The findings are elegantly summarised by Nicholas Carr (2014).
4. NTSB Vehicle Automation report Tempe, AZ, HWY18MH010, November 2019.

5. Some Uber insiders later told journalists that the company was fixated on a smooth ride that would impress senior executives, rather than safety (Uber insiders describe infighting and questionable decisions before its self-driving car killed a pedestrian. Business Insider, 19 November 2018, https://www.businessinsider.com/sources-describe-questionable-decisions-and-dysfunction-inside-ubers-self-driving-unit-before-one-of-its-cars-killed-a-pedestrian-2018-10).

6. Sensor supplier to self-driving Uber defends tech after fatality, Bloomberg, 23 March 2018, https://www.bloomberg.com/news/articles/2018-03-23/sensor-supplier-to-self-driving-uber-defends-tech-after-fatality.

7. Governor John Kasich, Ohio, 9 May 2018.

8. Governors Highway Safety Association, Pedestrian Traffic Fatalities by State, 2017 Preliminary Data, https://www.ghsa.org/sites/default/files/2018-03/pedestrians_18.pdf.

9. Declan McDowell-Naylor (2018) has drawn connections between Dahl's work and self-driving cars.

References

Carr, N. (2014). *The glass cage: Automation and us*. New York: W. W. Norton.

Dahl, R. A. (1961). *Who governs? Power and democracy in an American city*. New Haven: Yale University Press.

McDowell-Naylor, D. (2018). *The participatory, communicative, and organisational dimensions of public-making: Public engagement and the development of autonomous vehicles in the United Kingdom* (Unpublished PhD thesis). Royal Holloway, University of London.

CHAPTER 2

Innovation Is Not Self-Driving

A car crash is a product of countless causes. Individuals may in the moment make fateful decisions, but these decisions are enabled or constrained by the technologies around them, which are themselves the result of past choices. The built environment, the natural environment, the social environment and the regulatory environment all contribute to making technology what it is. The tangle of factors in these 'sociotechnical systems' confounds our ability to predict where technological innovation will take us next. But complexity is often used as an excuse for irresponsibility. If we want a democratic conversation about innovation, we first need to understand why technologies head in some directions and not others.

From a distance, technology seems to be driverless, evolving according to a set of unknown rules. The seemingly magical nature of new technologies has led some writers, including Kevin Kelly (2010), to conclude that technology is an autonomous and therefore uncontrollable system. Kelly writes, 'we can choose to modify our legal/political/economic assumptions to meet the ordained evolution ahead. But we cannot escape' from technological change.[1,2]

The sense that technology is out of control predates modern technology. It is a response to the imagined power of creation, a fear expressed in stories from Pygmalion and the Golem to Frankenstein and the Terminator. Technological optimists like Kevin Kelly see no reason to fear. They trust that the benefits of technology will in general outweigh any risks, and they don't think too much about who wins and who loses. For those in control

© The Author(s) 2020
J. Stilgoe, *Who's Driving Innovation?*,
https://doi.org/10.1007/978-3-030-32320-2_2

of innovation, it's a view that brings comfort. In 2018, Amazon CEO Jeff Bezos took the stage at a technology conference to point out the downsides of the technology that enabled him to become the world's richest person:

> Technologies always are two-sided. There are ways they can be misused as well as used. And this isn't new... We don't know the solutions to these problems yet, but we'll figure them out... Society develops an immune response eventually to the bad uses of new technology. But it takes time... The last thing we ever want to do is stop the progress of new technologies.[3]

Even in accentuating the negative, Bezos is claiming that technologies—*his* technologies—are inevitable, that any problems can and will be fixed and that they should only be governed by insiders. It's a common story, and it's one that most governments are happy to buy into. But the claim of inevitability is a form of power grab, an attempt to close the debate.

When political or corporate leaders talk about the 'fourth industrial revolution' and the need to position their nations or companies at its heart, they are contributing to this story of inevitability, attempting to wish technological change into existence by declaring that we are already in its midst. The performance of technological determinism is impressive, and it is carefully protected.[4] The people driving innovation expend substantial effort making their outputs appear inevitable and unproblematically beneficial, but still dependent on the determination and esoteric skills of heroic individuals. If we are to improve the governance of technology, this story needs to be challenged.

Faced with what seems to be a juggernaut of technological change, it is easy to forget that technologies are made by people. The historian Thomas Hughes (1993) proposed a form of soft technological determinism. He said that while new technologies are undeniably shaped by the needs, values and assumptions of human beings, they can build up momentum as they grow until it is not clear who is driving them. Marshall McLuhan concluded something similar: 'We become what we behold. We shape our tools, then our tools shape us'.[5] Winston Churchill, talking decades earlier in and about the Houses of Parliament, said, 'We shape our buildings, and afterwards our buildings shape us.' However, with buildings, we do not conclude that they were always destined to be there. To assume that buildings will appear, to forget about their foundations or their builders and to fixate on the quantity of buildings while ignoring their quality is a bad approach to policy.

The way that we think about the built environment can help us think about new technologies. Churchill was only half right. Some buildings do indeed impose themselves upon us, but some are designed to be more flexible. Architects and planners argue about the extent to which a building should respond to rather than try to shape people's lives. The high modernists that designed places like Brasilia claimed that well-planned cities could improve society. Their critics, including James Scott (1998) and Jane Jacobs (1961) argued that such plans were coercive and likely to fail. Stewart Brand (1995), a high priest of Silicon Valley techno-optimism, also took issue with the hubris of utopian architecture, writing, 'All buildings are predictions. All predictions are wrong'. Brand recommended following a strategy like that of a chess player: 'Favour moves that increase options; shy from moves that end well but require cutting off choices; work from strong positions that have many adjoining strong positions.'

This call for flexibility in our built environment mirrors a similar proposal for technologies, made by David Collingridge (1980). Collingridge identified a 'dilemma of control': we cannot predict the eventual shape or effects of complex technologies as they emerge and, by the time we know, it will be too late to change direction. Technological systems should, according to Collingridge, have flexibility built in, and we should we wary of technologies that lock us in to particular ways of life.

LOCKED INTO THE TECHNOSPHERE

The *Financial Times*'s word of the year in 2018 was 'Techlash'. It is only in the last couple of years that governments have woken up to Big Tech. The speed with which a few companies have grown has challenged policymakers' ability to understand the nature of this new corporate power. Some of the companies that are now among the world's largest are still adolescent. Facebook was founded in 2004. Google is only six years older. Having been treated with kid gloves, these companies' relationships with democratic politics are now becoming more fraught. After revelations about electoral interference, data breaches, privacy infringements, biased algorithms and tax avoidance, policymakers seem to finally be acknowledging previously unheeded concerns. But the path to good policy is not obvious. Governments are unsure how to make sense of new technologies. These companies are global and rarely liable for what happens on what they claim are just platforms.

When technologies go wrong, it is vital to learn from mistakes to avoid their repetition. But we should also take the opportunity to ask what happens when technologies succeed in their own terms. Facebook's power comes from lock-in. The company relies on the network effects of more than two billion active users binding each other into dependence as it, to use the company's slogan, 'helps you connect and share with the people in your life'. We use Facebook because others use Facebook.

The speed with which Facebook grew from a Harvard University project to a global network suggests it was meant to be. But its existence, its speed and its scale owe more to the law than to destiny or entrepreneurship. Facebook, YouTube and other online platforms became possible because of a rule originally designed by social conservatives as a protection against online pornography. The 1996 Communications Decency Act passed through the US Congress because of a concession that 'No provider or user of an interactive computer service shall be treated as the publisher or speaker of any information provided by another information content provider'. This law, and similar laws worldwide, absolves web sites from the responsibilities that newspapers and other publishers have.

In April 2018, Mark Zuckerberg was hauled before Congress to explain Facebook's involvement with the controversial data-mining company Cambridge Analytica. It was an awkward encounter. Once Congress had summoned up the will to hold the company to account, they were unsure how. The befuddled members of the Senate Judiciary Committee asked Zuckerberg to explain Facebook's business model. His response—'Senator, we run ads'—attracted attention both because of its simple honesty about the company's purpose and because of a suspicion that, as well as running ads, the company was running a para-state more powerful than many countries, doing politics by technological means. In response to speculation that Zuckerberg would one day run for president, one Facebook insider told a *Guardian* journalist, '[He] runs Facebook. Why would he want to run for president? He's already president of the world.'[6]

Earlier in 2018, a memo from a Facebook executive had been leaked to the press that revealed something about how the company considered its responsibilities:

> Maybe it costs a life by exposing someone to bullies. Maybe someone dies in a terrorist attack coordinated on our tools. And still we connect people. The ugly truth is that we believe in connecting people so deeply that anything that allows us to connect more people more often is *de facto* good.

Zuckerberg was forced to distance himself from this message, responding that Facebook 'never believed the ends justify the means. We recognize that connecting people isn't enough by itself. We also need to work to bring people closer together.'[7] But the real goal of Facebook was becoming increasingly clear: to grow as quickly as possible, at almost any cost. Facebook would say that it is so big because it works, but the main reason it works is that it is so big. Facebook's strategy, we now know, has been one of 'blitzscaling'. The company wanted, as quickly as possible, to become 'the operating system for our lives' (Vaidhyanathan 2018). Facebook, which began as an upstart, has become the establishment.

During the first dot com boom, US lawyer Lawrence Lessig saw how software was beginning to control our lives. To the question of how computer programmes should be governed, Lessing argued "Our choice is not between 'regulation' and 'no regulation.' The code regulates" (Lessig 2000). Lessig was sharpening an argument made in 1977 by Langdon Winner: technology constrains and enables our choices in much the same way as laws do, but the processes of debate and scrutiny that exist to shape our laws are largely absent when it comes to technology. We sleepwalk into the technological future (Winner 1977). We become enmeshed in technology that we struggle to understand and that we pretend we have chosen.

The human condition is inextricably technological. One rather quixotic attempt to audit the world's technology calculates the weight of the 'Technosphere' at 30 trillion tonnes. This include buildings, infrastructure and devices as well as the discarded substances that clutter the planet's surface, atmosphere and, since 1957, orbit (Zalasiewicz et al. 2017). We often think of the digital part of these technologies, the 'Infosphere' (Floridi 2014), as weightless. But the hardness of software is becoming increasingly clear. The 'cloud' is brought down to earth in banks of computing machinery that consume huge quantities of energy (Ensmenger 2018). Our lives have become dependent on a technological infrastructure that we are only starting to make sense of. And it is not clear who is responsible for any of it.

Negligence and Recklessness

The sociologist Ulrich Beck (1992) argued that the lines connecting innovation to its eventual consequences are so tangled and faint that we face a situation of 'organised irresponsibility'. When Mark Zuckerberg was a student, he could not have imagined the web site he built to allow students to connect with each other would attract more than two billion users.[8]

Jack Dorsey, the founder of Twitter, claims that he 'didn't fully predict or understand the real-world negative consequences'[9] of his platform, and we have some sympathy. Henry Ford could surely not have anticipated all of the hazards, the congestion or the sprawl that came with the technology he did so much to popularize. But this doesn't mean we should abandon efforts at 'anticipatory governance' (Guston 2014).

Most technologies fail to change the world and many successful ones get repurposed or reinvented as they are used and scaled up. Successful technologies are, according to Richard Sclove (1995), 'polypotent'. They are means to multiple ends. But they are also built with purposes in mind. Technologies such as Facebook are not the neutral 'platforms' that their creators would pretend them to be. If we want to consider the politics of a technology we should consider its obvious purposes as well as the other powers that it bestows. A hammer is designed to bang in nails; we don't blame the hammer if a murderer uses it to bludgeon someone to death. But, at the same time, most reasonable people can see the flaws in the excuse deployed by opponents of gun control: 'guns don't kill people, people do'.

The way we talk about technology is chronically lopsided. The positive effects of technology are often seen as 'intended', while the negative consequences are 'unintended'. It is too easy to explain away unintended consequences as the result of abuse by bad actors. Sheila Jasanoff (2016) argues that this asymmetry comes from the opacity of innovation. Technological design happens largely in private. When technologies have to be defended in public, their creators are able to get away with using 'unintended consequences' as an excuse.

In April 2018, Julian Knight, a British MP, tried to get Facebook to accept some blame, telling them, 'You aren't an innocent party wronged by the likes of Cambridge Analytica. You are the problem. Your company is the problem.' It was relatively easy for the company to deflect this attack, but the point remains: the issue with a particular technology may not be its unintended consequences, but its intended ones. For Facebook, infringements of privacy are a feature, not a bug. For YouTube, recommending extreme, divisive content is a feature, not a bug. For the manufacturers of social media apps and fixed-odds betting terminals, addiction is a feature, not a bug. For proponents of workplace automation and, in the future, artificial intelligence (AI), the deskilling and displacement of human labour is a feature, not a bug. It is naïve to suggest these effects are the result of mere negligence. They may be features not of a broken system, but of a world working as it has been designed.

When guns are used in school shootings, painkillers are implicated in an epidemic of opioid deaths, plastic waste fouls the oceans or cars endanger the lives of millions, it is insufficient to call such things 'unintended consequences'.[10] If we want to draw lines between thoughtlessness, negligence and recklessness, rather than asking whether consequences were intended, we should instead ask whether they were anticipated and, if not, why not?[11] Some effects are unanticipated because they are impossible to foresee; some are unanticipated on purpose; some are unanticipated by well-meaning, optimistic innovators. A separation of consequences into 'intended' and 'unintended' suggests a division of labour in which innovators get to define the good things and have plausible deniability while regulators mop up the bad.

In the world of tech, it is often unclear what the real intentions of innovators might be. We are used to start-ups setting out with the goal of solving a particular engineering problem and then pivoting once they realise there is money to be made. Sergey Brin and Larry Page (1998) wrote, in the paper that provided the recipe for Google, 'The goals of the advertising business model do not always correspond to providing quality search to users... we expect that advertising funded search engines will be inherently biased towards the advertisers and away from the needs of the consumers.' Google's business model could not survive such idealism. Its customers are now the advertisers, which means it has less reason to care about the interests of the people who use its services. This mismatch between benefits and costs, as Brin and Page realised, creates incentives for companies to obfuscate the real nature of the exchange. The people who are affected by the amassing of data may not be the beneficiaries of technology, nor even its users. Old ideas of economic exchange no longer work in what James Williams (2018) calls the 'Attention Economy'. Software is increasingly designed not to extract our money but to consume our time, which can then be sold to advertisers. In a world in which many products seem to cost nothing, attention has become a scarce resource.

The stories of both Facebook and Google are of tools that became, at scale, extraordinarily powerful attractors for advertising. Part of the reason why governments were so late to spot the downsides of Facebook is that they had swallowed the line that Facebook's purpose was to connect people. Its actual purpose was to expand its advertising business. The social contract on which innovators depend, and the individual contracts that they may have with users about, for example, what happens to their data, rest on the principle of informed consent. But as users we face what

Shoshana Zuboff (2019) calls a 'one-way mirror'; we aren't clear what these companies are doing or why they are so interested in us. It is often said that the challenge of regulation is one of catching up with technological change—law lags behind innovation. But in many cases the head start given to technology is deliberate. The US senators quizzing Facebook were widely derided for their technological incompetence. The bigger problem is that they chose not to care very much about what Facebook was doing. The gap between technology and regulation is a political choice.

TAKING THE WHEEL

In his last Presidential State of the Union address, Barack Obama said, 'Let's talk about the future… how do we make technology work for us, and not against us?' He had no time to provide an answer and his successor showed no interest in following it up.[12] The question remains hanging—seemingly too big for US policymakers to deal with.

For an emerging technology like AI, we can foresee some of the challenges even without predicting its eventual shape. In his advice to the French President, the mathematician Cedric Villani (2018) anticipated that AI would become the twenty-first century's power supply, much in the same way as electricity enabled twentieth century progress. Sundar Pichai, the CEO of Google, who employ more AI researchers than anyone, thinks that AI will be a technology 'more profound than, I don't know, electricity or fire.'[13] Notwithstanding the hype, we can agree that the owners of AI will command substantial political as well as technological power. Recognising the shape of this power and holding it to account presents a challenge of foresight and imagination for which governments are not well prepared. Worryingly, Vladimir Putin sees a new frontline for geopolitics: 'Artificial intelligence is the future, not only for Russia, but for all humankind. Whoever becomes the leader in this sphere will become the ruler of the world.'[14]

The companies that control software are now the world's biggest companies, and AI sits at the heart of each firm's strategy. Big companies like AI because of the economies of scale. For AI to make decisions in complex situations, it needs massive amounts of data, which limits the ability of small firms to compete. We should be concerned that the power supply is currently concentrated in the hands of so few, with so little government oversight. In the absence of good policymaking, AI is likely to turbocharge globalisation and the inequalities that come with it, while evading old forms of accountability and enabling new forms of oppression. Emmanuel Macron has recognised the need for Europe to develop alternative approaches to AI:

> The key driver should not only be technological progress, but human progress... In the US, it is entirely driven by the private sector... Chinese players collect a lot of data driven by a government whose principles and values are not ours. And Europe has not exactly the same collective preferences as US or China... if you want to manage your own choice of society, your choice of civilization, you [need] a say in designing and defining the rules of AI.[15]

The potential of self-driving car technology to contribute to human flourishing is vast. The story told by AI enthusiasts is that, if software could drive every car, the human error that accounts for almost all of the 1.3 million deaths that happen on the world's roads every year could be eradicated. Traffic could be made more efficient. Car parks could become parks. Taxis would cost a tenth of the price once human drivers are dispensed with.

If self-driving car innovation is well-governed, we can indeed imagine safer streets, less pollution, more liveable cities and mobility for people who have previously been shut out of transport because they are poor or disabled. However, if the people who are currently in control of innovation are left to their own devices, things are unlikely to end well. We could see companies following the money, leaving behind poor people or rural communities. We could see congestion worsen as zero-occupancy cars join single-occupancy cars to clog the streets. We could see competing standards and data-hoarding prevent the realisation of safety and efficiency benefits.

The first step is to recognise that, despite the substantial efforts to make particular technologies seem inevitable, there is a broad range of possible futures. Self-driving car technology could take various directions depending on ownership, regulation, business models, infrastructures, locations, user preferences, data-sharing or public resistance. We should certainly not presume that everyone will welcome the technology. There are plenty of examples of public opposition to technological proposals. The most well-known is the rejection of genetically modified foods in Europe. More recently, companies wishing to expand the use of fracking for natural gas in the UK have met well-organised and sustained protests. These opponents are often derided as 'anti-science' or 'anti-progress'. But just as with any other attempt to change the world, the developers of technology should expect and try to respond to opposition.

Learning by Doing

Sometimes, an untimely death can stun a promising technology for years, as was the case with gene therapy at the start of the twenty-first century. Sometimes, as with the first steam trains in the nineteenth century, even a high-profile casualty can be shrugged off as the price of progress.[16] Elaine Herzberg's death seems not to have stalled self-driving car innovation, although as one CEO inelegantly said, it has added 'a new data point'.[17] Uber themselves seem to have learned some lessons. If they haven't changed direction, they have certainly changed gear. Having previously insisted they were in a race to build a self-driving car, the company released a new Safety Report in November 2018 that came close to humility: 'For Uber, this is not a sprint: self-driving and human-driven vehicles will coexist on roadways for decades to come'.[18] The company upgraded their rules for testing, replacing a lone untrained occupant with two 'mission specialists' in each test car, and hired a former chair of the National Transportation Safety Board (NTSB), Christopher Hart, to advise them on safety. Policymakers should see Uber's misadventures as a harbinger of an undesirable future. The company has tried to learn its own lessons, but self-regulation is not enough.

There are limits to what can be done once technologies become embedded. As individual users, we may recognise our own ambivalence, alienation or addiction and take action. We may try to cut back our smartphone use, wean ourselves off social media, use alternative search engines or #Delete-Facebook.[19] But we are relatively powerless in our attempts to individually opt out of something to which we are collectively locked in. Those who do opt out are still affected by what rest of us are doing online. Collectively, it is even harder to act to control established technologies and encourage the development of alternatives.[20] Proposals to break up Big Tech companies or turn them into utilities are bold, but seem politically intractable. It is hard enough to tax them. As with the banking sector before the financial crisis, the build-up of unaccountable digital power has taken societies by surprise. Where governments have tried to hold Big Tech to account, there has been no discernible change of direction. The European Commission has fined Google billions of Euros for anticompetitive practices, but the company has taken this in its stride and responded that its near-monopoly was good for consumers. The European General Data Protection Regulation has been a rare moment in which digital technology companies have had to change some of their operations. Compared to the scale of the new digital infrastructures, such measures still seem too little, too late. For new technologies such as self-driving cars, there is a clear case for intervening earlier.

Collingridge's dilemma is not fatal. As with other areas of policy in which uncertainty is a given, the governance of technology is hard but possible. Just because governments have incomplete control, they should not concede to technological determinism. Our typical view of technology is refracted. Paul David (1991) calls it 'technological presbyopia': we overestimate the impact of a technology in the short run and underestimate its long-term ramifications. Policymakers can face the same problem. Geoff Mulgan, former Director of Policy for the UK Prime Minister, concluded that 'governments' usual optical distortion is that they overestimate the impact of short-term measures and underestimate how much can be changed over the longer term, with well-judged policies informed by hard evidence'.[21] Yes, technological change may have some features that are evolutionary and hard to control, but other ecosystems are shaped over time by good stewardship. One need only look at the different shapes that technologies take around the world. The historian Peter Norton (2008) has analysed the efforts made by the car lobby in the early twentieth century to make the transition to the petrol-driven car seem like a natural evolution. And yet, especially outside America, cities have engaged in diverse ways with the possibilities of the automobile. Taking a drive or a bike ride through Beijing, Los Angeles, Copenhagen or Kampala reveals a world of possible alternatives. Given the differences in transport systems that now exist across the world's cities, it would be surprising if self-driving cars ended up looking the same in all of them.

The question 'Who's driving?' is connected to another fundamental question of politics: 'Where are we going?' Technologies and governments both have profound long-term influence over our lives. But whereas in democracies we recognise that people can and should have a say, citizens could be excused for thinking that innovation is often done *to* them rather than *by* them or *for* them. A tiny minority—scientists, entrepreneurs or investors—may feel they can change things. For others, innovation feels driverless, leading to fatalism and alienation. As our futures come to be defined increasingly in technological terms, giving people a stake in their future means understanding and democratising the governance of technology.

NOTES

1. The quote is from a Kevin Kelly blog post, Was Moore's law inevitable? https://kk.org/thetechnium/was-moores-law/.
2. A critique of Kelly's determinism is in Morozov (2013).
3. Comments at Wired's 25th Anniversary Conference, reported in Amazon's Jeff Bezos: Social Media Inflames 'Identity Politics, Tribalism'. The Wrap, 15 October 2018, https://www.thewrap.com/jeff-bezos-social-media-makes-identity-politics-tribalism-worse/.
4. Technological determinism is the idea that 'machines make history' (Mackenzie 1984) and that they do so autonomously or "that social progress is driven by technological innovation, which in turn follows an 'inevitable' course" (Smith and Marx 1994).
5. This quote, usually attributed to McLuhan, was probably borrowed from his collaborator John Culkin. For more on this, see Bartlett (2018).
6. 'It's spot on': Facebook worker sees parallels with the circle, The Guardian, 2 May 2017, https://www.theguardian.com/technology/2017/may/02/facebook-the-circle-film-social-media-parallels.
7. Facebook VP wrote site's actions were 'de facto good'—even if they led to deaths, The Guardian, 30 March 2018, https://www.theguardian.com/technology/2018/mar/29/facebook-memo-mission-andrew-bosworth.
8. The Harvard Crimson university magazine reported on 9 February 2004, 'After about a week of coding, Zuckerberg launched thefacebook.com last Wednesday afternoon. The website combines elements of a standard House face book with extensive profile features that allow students to search for others in their courses, social organizations and Houses'.
9. Tweet, @jack, 1 March 2018, https://twitter.com/jack/status/969234278167949313.
10. Chris McGreal (2018) excoriates pharmaceutical companies who sold opioids for their deliberate ignorance as their products were overprescribed to US patients.
11. Langdon Winner (1977, p. 97) argued that a deliberate lack of precaution means 'unintended consequences are not *not* intended.'
12. It is worth noting that, before his election, Trump had told Breitbart, 'I have always been concerned about the social breakdown of our culture caused by technology'. Exclusive—Donald Trump to Breitbart Tech: Artificial Intelligence Creators, Users Should 'Consider Ethical and Moral Consequences'. Breitbart, 27 October 2015, https://www.breitbart.com/tech/2015/10/27/exclusive-donald-trump-to-breitbart-tech-artificial-intelligence-creators-users-should-consider-ethical-and-moral-consequences/.
13. Comments at an NBC/Recode Town Hall meeting, 19 January 2018.
14. Reported in 'Whoever leads in AI will rule the world': Putin to Russian children on Knowledge Day, RT, 1 September 2017, https://www.rt.com/news/401731-ai-rule-world-putin/.

15. Emmanuel Macron Talks to WIRED About France's AI Strategy. Wired, 31 March 2018, https://www.wired.com/story/emmanuel-macron-talks-to-wired-about-frances-ai-strategy/.
16. In 1999, Jesse Gelzinger was the first person to die in a clinical trial of a gene therapy treatment. In 1830, William Husskison, a local Member of Parliament, was run over and killed by George Stevenson's *Rocket* locomotive at the opening of the Liverpool and Manchester railway.
17. Jensen Huang, chief executive of Nvidia, quoted in Jensen Huang on the Uber Tragedy and Why Nvidia Suspended Testing. *IEEE Spectrum*, 30 March 2018, https://spectrum.ieee.org/view-from-the-valley/transportation/self-driving/jensen-huang-on-the-uber-tragedy-and-why-nvidia-suspended-testing.
18. Uber Advanced Technologies Group, A Principled Approach To Safety, 2018, https://uber.app.box.com/v/UberATGSafetyReport.
19. Technology company leaders have already begun to co-opt much of this reaction to their products. According to the *Financial Times*, at its 2018 Zeitgeist conference, Google gave each attendee a copy of a book—Silence in the Age of Noise—by explorer Erling Kagge that calls for people to escape technological distraction.
20. One prominent group that does this to an extreme degree is the Amish (Wetmore 2007).
21. My time in the engine room. *The Guardian*, 23 April 2005, https://www.theguardian.com/politics/2005/apr/23/election2005.labour.

References

Bartlett, J. (2018). *The people vs tech how the internet is killing democracy (and how we save it)*. London: Penguin Random House.
Beck, U. (1992). *Risk society: Towards a new modernity*. London: Sage.
Brand, S. (1995). *How buildings learn: What happens after they're built*. London: Penguin.
Brin, S., & Page, L. (1998). The anatomy of a large-scale hypertextual web search engine. *Computer Networks and ISDN Systems, 30*(1–7), 107–117.
Collingridge, D. (1980). *The social control of technology*. Milton Keynes: Open University Press.
David, P. A. (1991). Computer and dynamo: The modern productivity paradox in a not-too-distant mirror. In *Technology and productivity: The challenge for economic policy*. The Technology Economy Programmer (pp. 315–347). Paris, France: OECD Publishing.
Ensmenger, N. (2018). The environmental history of computing. *Technology and Culture, 59*(5), S7–S33.

Floridi, L. (2014). *The fourth revolution: How the infosphere is reshaping human reality.* Oxford: Oxford University Press.

Guston, D. H. (2014). Understanding 'anticipatory governance'. *Social Studies of Science, 44*(2), 218–242.

Hughes, T. P. (1993). *Networks of power: Electrification in western society, 1880–1930.* Baltimore: Johns Hopkins University Press.

Jacobs, J. (1961). *The death and life of great American cities.* New York, NY: Vintage.

Jasanoff, S. (2016). *The ethics of invention: Technology and the human future.* New York: W. W. Norton.

Kelly, K. (2010). *What technology wants.* New York: Penguin.

Lessig, L. (2000, January 1). Code is law: On liberty in cyberspace. *Harvard Magazine.* https://harvardmagazine.com/2000/01/code-is-law-html.

MacKenzie, D. (1984). Marx and the machine. *Technology and Culture, 25*(3), 473–502.

McGreal, C. (2018). *American overdose: The opioid tragedy in three acts.* London: Guardian Faber.

Morozov, E. (2013). *To save everything, click here: The folly of technological solutionism.* Public Affairs.

Norton, P. D. (2008). *Fighting traffic: The dawn of the motor age in the American city.* Cambridge: MIT Press.

Sclove, R. (1995). *Democracy and technology.* New York: Guilford Press.

Scott, J. C. (1998). *Seeing like a state: How certain schemes to improve the human condition have failed.* New Haven: Yale University Press.

Smith, M. R., & Marx, L. (Eds.). (1994). *Does technology drive history? The dilemma of technological determinism.* Cambridge: MIT Press.

Vaidhyanathan, S. (2018). *Antisocial media: How Facebook disconnects us and undermines democracy.* Oxford: Oxford University Press.

Villani, C. (2018). *For a meaningful artificial intelligence: Towards a French and European strategy.* https://www.aiforhumanity.fr/pdfs/MissionVillani_Report_ENG-VF.pdf.

Wetmore, J. M. (2007). Amish technology: Reinforcing values and building community. *IEEE Technology and Society Magazine, 26*(2), 10–21.

Williams, J. (2018). *Stand out of our Light: Freedom and resistance in the attention economy.* Cambridge: Cambridge University Press.

Winner, L. (1977). *Autonomous technology: Technics-out-of-control as a theme in political thought.* Cambridge: MIT Press.

Zalasiewicz, J., Williams, M., Waters, C. N., Barnosky, A. D., Palmesino, J., Rönnskog, A. S., et al. (2017). Scale and diversity of the physical technosphere: A geological perspective. *The Anthropocene Review, 4*(1), 9–22.

Zuboff, S. (2019). *The age of surveillance capitalism: The fight for a human future at the new frontier of power.* New York: Public Affairs.

CHAPTER 3

The Politics of Tech

PROBLEMS AND SOLUTIONS

For a self-driving car to learn to drive, it needs to be tested in the real world. Some companies, including Uber, have not hesitated to take their research outside. In 2009, when Google turned its attention to self-driving cars, the company began its tests hiding in plain sight on the roads of Silicon Valley. Larry Page, one of the Google founders, hired a team of America's leading roboticists and set them a target. If their car could do 101,000 self-driving miles on real roads, including routes like Lombard Street in San Francisco (the 'crookedest street in the world'), Page would give them a hefty bonus. Just as the team were nearing their goal, John Markoff, a technology reporter at *The New York Times*, was tipped off about this testing and asked Google for a comment. The secret engineering project quickly became a public relations exercise. In response to concerns about the safety of robot cars on public roads or the possibility of putting drivers out of work, Google recognised that it would not be adequate to justify the project as a fascinating engineering challenge or a way to further increase their market dominance. So began the process of self-driving car solutionism.

The word 'solutionism' was popularised by technology writer Evgeny Morozov (2013), building on a decades-old critique of 'technological fixes'.[1] For Morozov, the justification of technologies as solutions to social problems is intensely political: some problems get prioritised while others

© The Author(s) 2020
J. Stilgoe, *Who's Driving Innovation?*,
https://doi.org/10.1007/978-3-030-32320-2_3

are overlooked and, in making social problems amenable to engineering solutions, the problems are changed in ways that suit innovators.

A scan of recent tech news reveals solutionism in action. We have seen the rise and fall of Juicero, a company selling a Wi-Fi-connected fruit vice that the Washington Post called 'an expensive solution to a non-existent cold-pressed juice shortage'.[2] Soylent is a company that sells a food substitute inspired by 'the basic idea that nutrition shouldn't be difficult', with the eventual ambition of alleviating global food security. (The company later clarified that 'while Soylent can replace any meal, it is not intended to replace every meal'.)[3] Cryptocurrencies like Bitcoin are discussed by their evangelists as the solution to a litany of financial problems (many of which are conjured by a particular strain of libertarian thought), but they have failed to convince most people that they fulfil one of the basic roles of money: a store of value. The growing enthusiasm among technologists for the once fringe idea of transhumanism suggests a strong desire to solve the biggest problem of all: death. The attention devoted to such problems does not just distract from other, more important problems. It also obscures the problems that innovation itself creates. Bitcoin, for example, has, as well as contributing to reckless speculation and tax evasion, in the last few years consumed the same amount of electricity as some small countries (Ensmenger 2018).

40 years ago, Richard Nelson (1977) asked a question that remains relevant: How come the US, the world's richest country, was able to put a man on the moon but unable to solve the problems of its poorest citizens? His first response related to priorities: high-tech approaches get more than their fair share of political attention. His second answer was that not all problems are alike. According to Brenda Zimmerman and colleagues, some problems are simple, like following a recipe; some are complicated, like launching a rocket; others, like raising a child, are *complex* (Glouberman and Zimmerman 2002). Rocket science, it turns out, is not rocket science. The hard things about the moon landing were resolved with large amounts of money and manpower. The easy thing about the moon landing, from a sociological perspective, was that we could all agree on what the challenge was and we could all agree when it had been met. Social problems have additional layers of complexity. Poverty, pollution, famine, chronic disease and other targets of public policy are examples of what are now called 'wicked problems'. Rittel and Webber (1973) define wicked problems as having the following characteristics: they are unique, they are the symptoms of other problems, the causes are unclear or contested, attempts to tackle the

problem will change the problem and there is no opportunity for trial-and-error. For this reason, wicked problems have no right answers or neat solutions.[4] Even something that most would agree was a problem, such as cancer, raises a host of political questions: How much emphasis should be placed on personal responsibility relative to environmental causes? How much money and attention should the disease get relative to other conditions? How should resources be distributed between researching causes, finding cures and funding patient care?

'Technochauvinism' (Broussard 2018) is the tendency to privilege technological means over politics, which, according to John Gray, is 'the practical business of finding partial remedies for recurring ills' that are characterised by conflicting values.[5] For Cold War physicist and self-avowed technological fixer Alvin Weinberg, the Gordian knots of social problems provided an argument for rather than against technological fixes that can cut through complexity. The trouble is that technological fixes never make clean cuts. Weinberg (1966) knew that 'technological fixes do not get to the heart of the problem; they are at best temporary expedients.' Such 'solutions' do not solve anything. Instead, they reconfigure, hide, postpone or exacerbate real problems and trade-offs. And technologies create problems of their own. Technological optimists in the tradition of Weinberg would argue that in the future we will find ways to tackle antimicrobial resistance, biased algorithms and Bitcoin's energy usage, just as human ingenuity has historically 'fixed' the side-effects of past fixes. But even if this is true, it still doesn't get at the question of who gets to set the targets of innovation.

Everybody Needs a Thneed

Innovation can be seen as a form of conversation between needs and possibilities. We should be concerned when the conversation becomes too one-sided, with entrepreneurs defining both the problems and the solutions. Too often, the discussion starts with technologies rather than the problems that we would like technologies to address. Innovation scholar Everett Rogers (1962) realised that invention is often the mother of necessity:

> A need is a state of dissatisfaction or frustration that occurs when one's desires outweighs one's actualities (...) An individual may develop a need when he or she learns that an innovation exists. Therefore, innovations can lead to needs, as well as vice versa.

Deyan Sudjic, director of the Design Museum in London, talks about successful technologies as the 'things that we didn't know we couldn't do without' (Sudjic 2009, p. 60). Creating needs may be an easier way to sell products than solving problems, as Kodak recognised more than a century ago, advertising its cameras with the strapline: 'a vacation without a Kodak is a vacation wasted'.[6]

This dynamic was parodied in *The Lorax*, Dr. Seuss's story for children about the ecological destruction wrought by technology. In it, The Onceler, a faceless entrepreneur, develops a technology, the *Thneed* (a 'Fine-Something-That-All-People-Need'), that sells in vast quantities, causing pollution, misery and eventually bankruptcy. In a similar vein, there is a recent meme updating the hierarchy of needs originally devised by the psychologist Abraham Maslow. (It was Maslow who described the tendency, 'if the only tool you have is a hammer, to treat everything as if it were a nail'.) In Maslow's original scheme, high-level needs such as love and self-esteem were underpinned by basic needs of security, food and water. On the redrawn hierarchy, underneath all of these needs, someone has scrawled what they see as a more fundamental requirement: Wi-Fi.

Once needs are produced, they are hard to forget. For most people in rich countries, lives have already been reconfigured to make the Internet necessary. Even clear need-filling technologies create new expectations. Take the washing machine. It has with good reason been hailed as genuinely emancipatory, particularly for women, but it also changed social expectations about cleanliness and about who should be doing housework in middle-class households (Cowan 1983).

Technologies are often solutions in search of problems. For the Google engineers working on self-driving cars in 2009, the problem was relatively easy to find. There are than 1.3 million deaths every year as a result of cars, of which around 40,000 are in the US. By taking control away from fallible drivers and giving it to computers, the pitch is that self-driving cars would 'solve' the problem of road accidents.

This argument quickly unravels when we look at the alternative approaches we might take to road safety. If we compare statistics on road deaths, the international variation is huge, and the explanation is not to do with robot cars. In the US, there are more than ten road deaths per 100,000 people per year. The UK rate is around a third of this. Making roads and cars safer is possible using old-fashioned policies—upgrading infrastructure, enforcing laws, improving driver education and removing old cars from the road—but these come at a cost and they impinge upon the sense of freedom that is part of the automotive dream. There are cheap, available options, including speed limiters, seatbelt interlocks, and breathalysers that prevent the car from starting if a driver is over the alcohol limit. Such interventions, however, are seen as politically hard in the US. The fact that self-driving cars are seen as relatively easy tells us something about the bias towards new technologies.

The debate on artificial intelligence (AI) has revealed what technologist-turned-critic Jaron Lanier (2011) calls a 'bottomless ability to lower our standards to make information technology look good.' Humans debase themselves when presented with a story of what David Nye (1994) calls the 'technological sublime'. Within this story, the general public are cast in a very limited role: catch up, adapt, accept the inevitable and learn how to accommodate new technologies. If any individuals harbour concerns about the technology, one machine learning pioneer has advice: 'Your job in a world of intelligent machines is to keep making sure they do what you want, both at the input (setting the goals) and at the output (checking that you got what you asked for)' (Domingos 2015). The trouble is that a lone citizen would be almost powerless to do this, even if they agreed that it was a good use of their time.

To make driving—an intensely human, conversational activity—into a solvable problem, the task needs to be narrowed and rationalised to the point at which humans resemble what some ethicists have called 'drunk robots' (Sparrow and Howard 2017). A 2016 piece in *Time Magazine* insisted that 'the computer is simply a better driver than a human,'[7] following a logic that is neatly captured in this quote from business school professor and self-driving car enthusiast Ajay Agrawal:

> Six years ago, experts were saying we would never have a driverless car on a city street in our lifetime. Until it was converted into a prediction problem... the prediction is 'what would a good human driver do?'... Humans have data coming in through the sensors - the cameras on our face and the microphones on the sides of our heads - and the data comes in, we process the data with our monkey brains and then we take actions and our actions are very limited: we can turn left, we can turn right, we can brake, we can accelerate.[8]

This description misrepresents both human driving and self-driving technologies, but it's a simplification that serves a purpose. Elon Musk would agree with it. He told a conference in 2015, 'You can't have a person driving a 2-ton death machine... It's too dangerous.'[9] When humans compare themselves to an idealised machine, the imperfections stand out. Even though humans are the only control devices ever to have successfully driven cars, some are ready to make the argument that driving should be banned.

GROWING FOR THE MACHINE

If we want to understand the politics of today's and tomorrow's technologies, we should look back to the technologies that are now regarded as part of society's inevitable industrialisation and ask who benefitted and why. The philosopher of technology Langdon Winner asks us to consider the tomato. The tomatoes on a twenty-first century supermarket shelf are the way they are because of a set of organisational and technological choices. The technologisation of the tomato was extraordinarily rapid. In 1960, the tomato fields of California contained fruit in a variety of shapes and sizes and were picked by hand; mostly by the hands of tens of thousands of *braceros* (immigrant Mexican workers). By 1970, almost all of California's tomatoes were harvested by machines.[10]

The machine that enabled the industrialisation of tomato farming came from a collaboration between a fruit breeder and an aeronautical engineer at the University of California, Davis, in the 1940s. In one pass, the tomato harvester could cut a row of plants, shake the fruit from their stalks and drop them into a trailer. Humans were required only to drive the machine, maintain it, check the tomatoes and throw out any dirt, stalks or small animals that ended up in the trailer. After early attempts to get the fruit to survive the journey from field to trailer intact, the researchers realised that, for the tomato harvester to work as intended, the tomato itself had to be tougher and less tasty—good for ketchup and processed food; bad for salads. Fields had to be rectangular, flat and well-irrigated. Farmers had to learn how to, in the words of one of the engineers, 'grow for the machine'.[11] Each device was expensive but, if a farm was big enough to afford one, it could dramatically cut costs.

In the late 70s, when Winner was writing, a group representing migrant labourers—California Rural Legal Assistance—were trying to sue UC Davis on the grounds that public money was being spent on research that was hurting employment and helping corporations. Winner concluded that the university researchers who designed the machines were not trying to put anyone out of work or line farm owners' pockets, but the winners from this new system were clear—large farms that could afford the machinery. The losers were the labourers who lost their jobs and the small farms who couldn't afford to invest. Consumers got cheap, abundant tomatoes, but they were different tomatoes. Nor is this a simple story of robots taking jobs. The tomato machines were available for a number of years before they were deployed widely. They only became popular once policies were introduced to expel cheap immigrant labour. This allowed US farm workers to earn more, but increased farmers' incentives to automate and turn their fields over to tomatoes.

The debate about automation and labour is nothing new. We can look back to the Luddites in the nineteenth century. Their cause was not a hatred of technology (although that is normally how the label is used today) but a fear about the balance of power between workers and their bosses. With the spread of industrialisation and the economic returns that came with it, some were more optimistic. In the twentieth century, John Maynard Keynes thought that 'technological unemployment', caused by 'economising the use of labour outrunning the pace at which we can find new uses for labour' (Keynes 1933, p. 3) would be inevitable, opening up the possibility of more leisurely lifestyles and a shorter working week. Others were sceptical that productivity benefits would be shared with workers.

The contemporary debate about AI has lost some of this nuance. Maybe if we adopted an earlier term for AI—'the mechanisation of thought'—we might have a clearer sense of who is doing what. In the 1970s, one of the most strident and lucid critiques of AI came from an insider, Joseph Weizenbaum, the creator of the first chatbot. His book was not about what computers could do, but about what they should do. His aim was to reassert the value of human thought at a time in which, as I discuss in the next chapter, the assumption among some AI researchers was that computers would soon make humanity redundant. His argument was not just that computers will never be able to do everything humans do, but that we should resist the urge to turn human judgements into simple decisions. As with tomato harvesters, new technologies do not have to become superhuman for those in power to make use of them to replace labour. Weizenbaum's concern was not with computers becoming more human, but with humans becoming more computerised. He made use of a contemporary account of working Americans from the oral historian Studs Terkel:

For the many, there is a hardly concealed discontent. The blue-collar blues is no more bitterly sung than the white-collar moan. 'I'm a machine,' says the spot-welder. 'I'm caged,' says the bank teller, and echoes the hotel clerk. 'I'm a mule,' says the steelworker. 'A monkey can do what I do,' says the receptionist. 'I'm less than a farm implement,' says the migrant worker. 'I'm an object,' says the high-fashion model. Blue collar and white call upon the identical phrase: 'I'm a robot.'[12]

It is impossible to aggregate the concerns about the quality of work expressed here, or those expressed by the people working precariously in Amazon's highly-automated delivery centres or Facebook's content moderation farms, to calculate the quantities of jobs in a future economy. In the case of the tomato harvester, the new jobs in operating and maintaining the machinery could not replace the lost jobs in picking, but jobs were created in other parts of the economy. In the second half of the twentieth century, company managers began to understand the negative impact on their workers of 'scientific management' or 'Taylorisation', which prized efficiency at all costs. The lesson, which risks being lost in the debate about AI, was that automation should be wisely deployed to reduce drudgery and enable creative work; good jobs are not reducible to a set of tasks.

Most economists conclude that technological change enables a net creation of jobs, but have less to say about the quality and distribution of these jobs. David Autor (2019) is an exception, using labour data to understand the unevenness of technological progress. His conclusion is that the future digital economy will see growing inequality, with money to be made at the top and bottom of the income distribution, but less in between. Autor already sees a rending of the labour force into 'frontier workers' who are in control of the new technology, 'wealth workers' serving the needs of the rich and 'last mile workers' doing unskilled tasks like package delivery. The wages of this last category of jobs are flatlining while others are growing. Over the last few decades, almost all of the value added by increased productivity has gone to the owners of factories rather than their workers (Autor and Salomons 2018). The hard truth is that technology, in the absence of progressive social policy, tends to widen the gap between the people with money, skills and connections who are best able to take advantage of its novelties, and others.[13]

If we buy even partially the predictions about the speed of development of driverless vehicles, the consequences for jobs could be profound. Truck driving remains one of the best-paid jobs in the US that doesn't require a college degree. Some companies have tried to head off the concerns. Starsky robotics, who are developing self-driving trucks, say 'The problem we're addressing is the shortage of truck drivers'.[14] Unions and current or future drivers may not agree with the company's diagnosis or its priorities.

For AI, there is a concern, boosted by some rather speculative research, that the robots are coming for middle-class as well as working-class jobs.[15] Lawyers, doctors and accountants are under threat from superhuman AIs, we are told. However, such speculation focuses too much on the imagined technology and not enough on the politics. Langdon Winner argues that those in power will often develop and make use of technology even if it is demonstrably worse than the human alternative. (This will be familiar to anyone that has experienced an automated telephone service or super-market self-checkout.)[16] For Winner, 'It is obvious that technologies can be used in ways that enhance the power, authority, and privilege of some over others' (Winner 1980). Others forget this. AI will, if left unchecked, be a force multiplier for inequality, but the real issue is not that AI will be used because it is cleverer than a human; it will be used because it is cheaper and less demanding than a human. And when it is used, the other qualities of human workers that seem inefficient, including empathy, imagination, accountability and flexibility, may be pushed aside. For humans to be put out of work in the ways assumed in models of AI and employment, the world would have to change in ways that are not just technological. If technology becomes an easy scapegoat for job losses, the people making the decisions will evade responsibility.

ALGORITHMIC OPPRESSION

Technological innovation is double-edged. The justification is often that the benefits outweigh the risks, but the issue is that the people benefitting are not normally the ones bearing the burdens of innovation. If we consider the proliferation of services online, the benefits to consumers are immediately apparent: free and convenient tools like email, search, maps and social networks. Our realisation of the costs lags far behind. When data are harvested, aggregated and used to build models from which inferences are made, the real beneficiaries are the companies large enough to have economies of scale.

The algorithmic ideal is that mathematics can not only engineer efficiency but also filter out injustice: as data grows in scale, speed and scope, services can become more personalised, more accessible and fairer. It should be easier in principle for people to get what they need when they need it. Except that, in practice, we have seen some examples that suggest the opposite. People in privileged positions may feel that the decisions they make are newly empowered by data. For others, public and private sector institutions that claim to know them better than they know themselves are making choices on their behalf or that affect them indirectly, which can turn out to be oppressive.

Virginia Eubanks (2018) has studied the use of algorithmic tools by public sector agencies that mean well but are struggling to allocate their scarce resources. Fateful decisions about whether someone will be allocated social housing, investigated for child neglect or granted welfare payments are being made on behalf of individuals based upon a range of variables, each of which put people into categories. In one case that Eubanks analyses, the city of Los Angeles gathered intimate data about sexual history in order to identify and house the most vulnerable people, but there was so little housing available that the data was of more use to the police, who used it to focus their investigations and criminalise homeless people. In a sense, this is an old pattern of bureaucratic order, but the algorithms act as what Eubanks calls 'empathy overrides', outsourcing difficult decisions while pretending to encode fairness. This perpetuates a system that Eubanks likens to a 'digital poorhouse', in which the state manages the effects of poverty rather than tackling its causes. And when technologies are justified as solutions to injustice, questions of accountability and due process can be overlooked.

A common assumption in data science is that algorithmic bias can be fixed, and it can be fixed with more data. But the politics is inescapable. Mathematics cannot solve for fairness, not least because people will always disagree on what counts as 'fair' (Olhede and Wolfe 2018). Engineers can choose not to cut data by categories such as race that we agree should not be the basis for discrimination, but the algorithms will remain discriminatory. Indeed, they are designed to discriminate, to put people in categories in order to achieve a goal. Personalisation and accuracy should not necessarily be the priority. There are some social institutions, including the British National Health Service, which I will return to in Chapter 5, that were designed and have evolved to collectivise risk, prioritising solidarity over efficiency and personalisation. The accountability of systems is about more than openness. Transparency may help, but it is not sufficient to know how algorithms work. Institutions also need to be explicit about why new technologies are being used if they want to weed good technology from bad.

The examples of algorithmic injustice that we are already seeing should make us rethink the normal story about new technologies and inequality. In the past, the assumption has been that technological benefits will trickle down from innovators and early adopters to the masses. The problem was characterised as one of access.[17] At the start of the twenty-first century, concerns about the 'digital divide' were followed by optimism as people in poor countries, often using mobile phones, were able to get online. But the problems analysed by Eubanks are not to do with access. Many of the people she describes have plenty of access to technology but no control over its use. Cathy O'Neil (2017) paints a bleak future in which 'The privileged, we'll see time and again, are processed more by people, the masses by machines.' The bigger problem is not the speed or extent of technological gentrification, but the purposes and direction of innovation.

We can find some cause for optimism in the recent movements among tech workers to question their companies' research agendas. In 2018, 3000 highly-skilled Google employees realised their collective power and forced the company to back out of 'Project Maven', an attempt by the US military to use Google's AI to improve the targeting of weapons. Later that year, employees joined lawyers and civil rights activists in calling for a cancellation of a search engine that would allow the Chinese government to censor searches. Their open letter said, 'We object to technologies that aid the powerful in oppressing the vulnerable, wherever they may be.'[18] Unfortunately, such technologies are far more widespread than the Google employees realise.

TECHNOLOGY FOR THE 1%

In 2015, one Silicon Valley insider, exasperated at what he saw as vacuous innovation, tweeted 'Tech culture is focused on solving one problem: What is my mother no longer doing for me?'[19] His comment resonated because of a growing awareness that the priorities of Silicon Valley innovators may not match those of the rest of the world or even the rest of the US.

According to one Facebook insider, the motivation driving disruptive innovation is a '"fuck you" to those in power'.[20] The assumption is that new technologies and smart, well-meaning people will be able to cut through the sclerotic established hierarchies and enable social change from which everyone will benefit. In his landmark book on economic inequality, Thomas Piketty (2014) explained the reasoning—'the progress of technological rationality is supposed to lead automatically to the triumph of human capital over financial capital and real estate, capable managers over fat cat stockholders, and skill over nepotism'—before going on to explain why this doesn't happen.

Tim O'Reilly, a guru of Silicon Valley, told *Wired Magazine* in 2016, as if it were incontrovertible, 'If a company creates more value than it captures, it decreases inequality, no matter how rich the founders become'.[21] The scale of the delusion is remarkable. In the absence of any outside involvement, science and technology will tend reinforce rather than close inequalities. As Edward Woodhouse and Dan Sarewitz (2007) have written, 'To expect otherwise would require that science agendas differ from every other human enterprise'. Archaeological studies (e.g. Kohler et al. 2017) have explored in detail the technological means with which inequality has widened since Neolithic times, as societies shifted from hunting and gathering to farming. Farming allowed for the concentration and passing on of wealth, largely in the form of land. And industrialisation allowed for further increases in inequality.

In Silicon Valley, the winners and losers from the new economy are clearly visible on the streets, as Douglas Rushkoff (2016), Richard Walker (2018) and others attest. And economists like Branko Milanovic and Erik Brynjolfsson have concluded that technological inequality is also visible in the statistics, explaining much of the recent disparity in income in rich countries. Digital technologies have enabled a winner-takes-all pattern that has seen the income share of the richest 1% increase (Guellec and Paunov 2017) while the average worker in rich countries has seen their income stagnate.[22]

A second part of the Silicon Valley ideal is that technology will 'democratise' the tools of innovation, giving people from all walks of life the ability to shape the future. Here again, the evidence doesn't fit the story. A study found that the children of the richest 1% of Americans were ten times more likely to become inventors than those from the bottom 50%, even when results in maths tests were taken into account (Bell et al. 2017). As Michael Young (1958) predicted, 'meritocracy' (a term he coined pejoratively) would in fact see the creation new dynasties, with the additional problem that these groups were more likely to believe that they deserved their success.

WHO BENEFITS?

Problems that get chosen and solutions that are offered reflect the values of the people involved in innovation. It is easy to mock companies like Soylent, whose founder saw the need to eat as such a hassle that he was driven to engineer an alternative. Such companies seem to confirm the suspicion that the people who've got it made will just keep making things for themselves. But there are plenty of counterexamples of technologies that have genuinely increased human welfare and freedom: the car has enabled the mobility of millions, with all of the opportunities that brings; vaccines have eradicated and controlled diseases, often in places with threadbare healthcare systems; new food crops and ways of growing them have boosted yields and allowed farmers to develop livelihoods; for farmers and other small business owners in Sub-Saharan Africa, where infrastructure is poor, mobile phones have led to dramatic improvements in productivity by providing access to information about markets and weather; improvements in solar panels and wind turbines have made clean energy a realistic goal.

As individual examples, these and myriad others offer reason for optimism. And yet, in general, we still see stark mismatches between innovation and needs. The vast bulk of the world's biomedical R&D money, from public as well as private sources, is spent on addressing the concerns of the rich world, while diseases prevalent in poor countries are neglected. The emancipatory potential of technology will never be realised without political as well as entrepreneurial effort.

If we were able to know more in advance about who benefitted from technological change, we would be able to have an informed discussion about its politics. The lines between innovation and its eventual effects are hazy, and the ways that we measure progress, including statistics such as Gross Domestic Product, hide the unevenness of change. We do not know enough about who benefits from what sorts of innovation, but we can be fairly sure that if we don't keep looking, existing inequalities will be exacerbated and, by the time the winners and losers are revealed, the technology may already be locked in.

For Paul David (1991), policymakers' skewed view of technology means they fail to ask political questions about the future that enable good choices in the present:

> There is an understandable inclination to concentrate on the future, holding onto the prospect of dramatic improvements in the material circumstances of the mass of humanity without having to contemplate overt conflicts that

would be provoked by the purposive redistribution of existing wealth. In the long run it may be a functional response on the part of the modern industrial democracies to try and direct the energies of society away from redistributive struggles and toward the cooperative conquest of the 'endless frontier' of science.

A recent survey suggests that members of the British public do not buy the story of the endless frontier: only 16% of people think that the benefits of future technology will be shared evenly across society.[23] For innovators and policymakers, this should be a wake-up call. A naïve view of technologies as mere tools and tech firms as just like other firms is no longer sustainable. Technological innovation should not be seen as an end in itself. In the next chapter, I argue that a more critical approach to claims about the future benefits of technology will enable policymakers to play an active role both in using technology to tackle society's real problems and in tackling the problems of technology.

Notes

1. Morozov borrowed the word from the Canadian Economist Gilles Paquet, who described a worldview that sees only 'puzzles to which there is a solution, rather than problems to which there may be a response'.
2. Juicero shows what's wrong with Silicon Valley thinking, Christine Emba, Washington Post, 24 April 2017, https://www.washingtonpost.com/blogs/post-partisan/wp/2017/04/24/juicero-shows-whats-wrong-with-silicon-valley-thinking/.
3. It is impossible to mention Soylent without noting that the company got its name from a 1973 sci fi film—Soylent Green—in which the twist was that people's diets were based on human remains.
4. Kelly Levin et al. (2012) have argued that climate change is actually a 'super-wicked problem', further complicated by its global scale, its urgency and lack of clear governance.
5. Philosophies of history are rationalisations for mass murder: An interview with John Gray, The Quietus, 28 April 2018, https://thequietus.com/articles/24484-john-gray-interview-seven-types-of-atheism.
6. Thanks to Harro van Lente for this example.
7. Matt Vella: Why you shouldn't be allowed to drive. Time, 7 March 2016, https://time.com/magazine/us/4236955/march-7th-2016-vol-187-no-8-u-s/.
8. AI economics: How cheaper predictions will change the world, Ajay Agrawal, YouTube, 4 May 2018, https://www.youtube.com/watch?v=YRzGSp_bO1M.

9. Musk: Someday, driving a car will be illegal, CNBC, 17 March 2017, https://www.cnbc.com/2015/03/17/musk-someday-driving-a-car-will-be-illegal.html.
10. The economic history of the tomato harvester is explained by Clemens et al. (2018).
11. Quoted in The Tomato Harvester, Boom California, https://boomcalifornia.com/2013/06/24/thinking-through-the-tomato-harvester/.
12. Quoted in Weizenbaum (1976).
13. Some of the few other prominent economists asking such questions are Erik Brynjolfsson and Andrew McAfee (2014).
14. Why our company's trucks won't carry lidar, IEEE Spectrum, 28 November 2018, https://spectrum.ieee.org/cars-that-think/transportation/self-driving/why-our-companys-trucks-wont-carry-lidar.
15. The research by Frey and Osborne (2017) has been much cited.
16. An analysis of the work created by ostensibly labour-saving machinery is in Mateescu and Elish (2019).
17. Hal Varian, Google's chief economist has a rule, for which the exceptions are almost overwhelming, that captures this view: 'A simple way to forecast the future is to look at what rich people have today; middle-income people will have something equivalent in 10 years, and poor people will have it in an additional decade.' Varian, H, 15 August 2011, "Micromultinationals Will Run the World", https://foreignpolicy.com/2011/08/15/micromultinationals-will-run-the-world/.
18. We are Google employees. Google must drop Dragonfly, 27 November 2018, https://medium.com/@googlersagainstdragonfly/we-are-google-employees-google-must-drop-dragonfly-4c8a30c5e5eb.
19. Aziz Shamim, Tweet, 4 May 2015, https://twitter.com/azizshamim/status/595285234880491521?lang=en.
20. This quote if from an anonymous friend of Mark Zuckerberg to The New Yorker. Can mark Zuckerberg fix Facebook before it breaks democracy? The New Yorker, 17 September 2018, https://www.newyorker.com/magazine/2018/09/17/can-mark-zuckerberg-fix-facebook-before-it-breaks-democracy.
21. Hey Silicon Valley: President Obama has a to-do list for you, Wired Magazine, 18 October 2016, https://www.wired.com/2016/10/obama-six-tech-challenges/.
22. We should acknowledge that many of those whose incomes have not increased have still seen increases in standards of living through access to cheaper and better technologies.
23. Public views on technology futures, survey by Demos/Opinium, 2017, https://www.demos.co.uk/project/public-views-on-technology-futures/.

REFERENCES

Autor, D. (2019, January 4). Work of the past, work of the future, Richard T. Ely Lecture, AEA Annual Meeting Atlanta. https://economics.mit.edu/files/16724.

Autor, D., & Salomons A. (2018, Spring). *Is automation labor-displacing? Productivity growth, employment, and the labor share.* BPEA Conference Draft.

Bell, A. M., Chetty, R., Jaravel, X., Petkova, N., & van Reenen, J. (2017). *Who becomes an inventor in America? The importance of exposure to innovation* (No. w24062). National Bureau of Economic Research.

Broussard, M. (2018). *Artificial unintelligence: How computers misunderstand the world.* Cambridge: MIT Press.

Brynjolfsson, E., & McAfee, A. (2014). *The second machine age: Work, progress, and prosperity in a time of brilliant technologies.* New York: W. W. Norton.

Clemens, M. A., Lewis, E. G., & Postel, H. M. (2018). Immigration restrictions as active labor market policy: Evidence from the Mexican bracero exclusion. *American Economic Review, 108*(6), 1468–1487.

Cowan, R. (1983). *More work for mother: The ironies of household technology from the open hearth to the microwave.* New York: Basic Books.

David, P. A. (1991). Computer and dynamo: The modern productivity paradox in a not-too-distant mirror. In *Technology and productivity: The challenge for economic policy.* The Technology Economy Programmer (pp. 315–347). Paris, France: OECD Publishing.

Domingos, P. (2015). *The master algorithm: How the quest for the ultimate learning machine will remake our world.* New York: Basic Books.

Ensmenger, N. (2018). The environmental history of computing. *Technology and Culture, 59*(5), S7–S33.

Eubanks, V. (2018). *Automating inequality: How high-tech tools profile, police, and punish the poor.* New York: St. Martin's Press.

Frey, C. B., & Osborne, M. A. (2017). The future of employment: How susceptible are jobs to computerisation? *Technological Forecasting and Social Change, 114,* 254–280.

Glouberman, S., & Zimmerman, B. (2002). *Complicated and complex systems: What would successful reform of medicare look like?* (Discussion Paper No. 8). Commission on the Future of Health Care in Canada.

Guellec, D., & Paunov, C. (2017). *Digital innovation and the distribution of income* (No. w23987). National Bureau of Economic Research.

Keynes, J. M. (1933). Economic possibilities for our grandchildren. In *Essays in persuasion.* London: Palgrave Macmillan.

Kohler, T. A., Smith, M. E., Bogaard, A., Feinman, G. M., Peterson, C. E., Betzenhauser, A., et al. (2017). Greater post-Neolithic wealth disparities in Eurasia than in North America and Mesoamerica. *Nature, 551*(7682), 619.

Lanier, J (2011). *You are not a gadget: A manifesto.* New York: Vintage.

Levin, K., Cashore, B., Bernstein, S., & Auld, G. (2012, May 23). Overcoming the tragedy of super wicked problems: Constraining our future selves to ameliorate global climate change. *Policy Sciences, 45*(2), 123–152. https://doi.org/10.1007/s11077-012-9151-0.

Mateescu, A., & Elish, M. C. (2019). *AI in context: The labor of integrating new technologies.* Data & Society Research Institute. Accessed at https://apo.org.au/node/217456 on 21 March 2019.

Morozov, E. (2013). *To save everything, click here: The folly of technological solutionism.* Public Affairs.

Nelson, R. R. (1977). *The moon and the ghetto: An essay on public policy analysis.* New York: W. W. Norton.

Nye, D. E. (1994). *American technological sublime.* Cambridge: MIT Press.

Olhede, S. C., & Wolfe, P. J. (2018). The growing ubiquity of algorithms in society: Implications, impacts and innovations. *Philosophical Transactions of the Royal Society A: Mathematical, Physical and Engineering Sciences, 376*(2128), art. 20170364.

O'Neil, C. (2017). *Weapons of math destruction: How big data increases inequality and threatens democracy.* New York: Broadway Books.

Piketty, T (2014). *Capital in the twenty-first century.* Cambridge: Harvard University Press.

Rittel, H. W., & Webber, M. M. (1973). Dilemmas in a general theory of planning. *Policy Sciences, 4*(2), 155–169.

Rogers, E. M. (1962). *Diffusion of innovations.* New York: Simon & Schuster.

Rushkoff, D. (2016). *Throwing rocks at the Google bus: How growth became the enemy of prosperity.* New York: Penguin.

Sparrow, R., & Howard, M. (2017). When human beings are like drunk robots: Driverless vehicles, ethics, and the future of transport. *Transportation Research Part C: Emerging Technologies, 80,* 206–215.

Sudjic, D. (2009). *The language of things: Understanding the world of desirable objects.* New York: W. W. Norton.

Walker, R. (2018). *Pictures of a gone city: Tech and the dark side of prosperity in the San Francisco Bay Area.* Oakland: PM Press.

Weinberg, A. M. (1966). Can technology replace social engineering? *Bulletin of the Atomic Scientists, 12*(10), 4–8.

Weizenbaum, J. (1976). *Computer power and human reason: From judgment to calculation.* San Francisco: W. H. Freeman.

Winner, L. (1980). Do artifacts have politics? *Daedalus, 109,* 121–136.

Woodhouse, E., & Sarewitz, D. (2007). Science policies for reducing societal inequities. *Science and Public Policy, 34*(2), 139–150.

Young, M. (1958). *The rise of the meritocracy.* London: Pelican.

CHAPTER 4

In Dreams Begins Responsibility

In 2017, Elon Musk claimed that, by the end of the year, a Tesla would be able to drive 'from a parking lot in California to a parking lot in New York. No controls touched at any point during the entire journey'.[1] At the time, Tesla customers could pay an extra $8000 for 'Full self-driving capability' in their new cars. As of 2019, this capability and the promised coast-to-coast drive remain unfulfilled. In 2018, when he was challenged by the journalist Lesley Stahl on his failure to meet deadlines, Musk laughed it off, saying 'Punctuality's not my strong suit'. When Stahl suggested that some would call this lying, Musk replied 'people should not ascribe to malice that which can easily be explained by stupidity... I'm dumb at predicting dates. It doesn't mean I'm untruthful.'[2]

Tesla is an exquisitely Californian construction. It embodies what Richard Barbrook and Andy Cameron (1996) called the 'Californian ideology', a sun-bleached blend of progressive utopianism and techno-libertarianism. After Musk took over the company, his 'Master Plan' was to sell a sports car, the profits from which would fund the development of affordable electric cars and solar panels that would transform driving and electricity generation. The plan has not come off as promised, but, despite

'In Dreams Begins Responsibility' is taken from Responsibilities, a book of poems by W. B. Yeats.

© The Author(s) 2020
J. Stilgoe, *Who's Driving Innovation?*,
https://doi.org/10.1007/978-3-030-32320-2_4

some very public setbacks, Tesla have indeed disrupted the market for cars and given momentum to new possibilities for transport. If Musk, described by a Washington Post journalist as Tesla's 'chief executive, visionary and hype man',[3] and other Silicon Valley prophets are to deserve our credit, we could also ask what responsibilities they have for the promises they make and then break.

The Audacity of Hype

In an uncertain world, technological hype is a way to make claims about the future that seem rooted in scientific rigour. If technologies succeed and become embedded in our everyday lives, we take them for granted and they fade into the background. Nascent technologies, however, must compete for our attention. They must be made visible despite their non-existence. The paradox is therefore that the technological possibilities that are furthest off tend to be the most hyped. Novelty is seductive. New technologies can seem pristine, untainted by past associations. It is only when promises meet the real world that the myriad complications that might dampen excitement are revealed (Borup et al. 2006).

Consultants are on hand to back-up predictions with data. One firm, Gartner, draws up a 'Hype Cycle' every year that plots technologies' journeys from promise to reality. In 2015, Gartner had autonomous vehicles (self-driving cars) at the peak of hype, but calculated that they were between five and ten years away. In 2016, they concluded that the hype was subsiding, but the technology was now more than ten years away, where it has stayed in subsequent years. Gartner's task is complicated by the fact that technologies do not arrive fully-formed, for everyone, everywhere. Many technologies fail and the rest change as they become successful.

Technological hype is not just exaggeration, nor is it idle speculation; it is an act of persuasion. We should therefore pay close attention to who is predicting what and why. A study of Gartner and similar organisations by two sociologists found that consultants are well aware that they are making rather than just predicting the future. One analyst admitted, 'That is how you know what is coming next: because you are making it come next' (Pollock and Williams 2016, p. 3).

The making of a claim about the future is an attempt to stake a claim on the future and to foreclose alternatives. With self-driving cars, hype is used to stake a claim on present day roads too. Uber, by exaggerating the potential of their technology, were asserting a right to use Arizona's road-space for their tests. The aim is to change the present such that a prophecy can become self-fulfilling. The use of science makes such claims more persuasive. Medical science is particularly susceptible to hype. Patients are vulnerable and even the slightest chance of a treatment's success can skew the assessment. The emergence of over-hyped industries around egg-freezing, cord-blood banking, cryonics and experimental regenerative medicine can be explained in part by the power of hope.

The incentives to hype are clear. There is competition for the attention, skills, finance and other resources necessary to realise technological visions. Companies and policymakers know that the future is profoundly unpredictable, and yet they must organise resources in the present in a way that suggests the future is under control. As Hannah Arendt described, we must all navigate the 'ocean of future uncertainty' by making promises in the present, 'to create reliability and predictability that would otherwise be out of reach.'[4] Hype is not all bad. In a world in which technology has become a new currency, but the uncertainties of innovation are ever-present, hype is a way to build social capital, with the hope that financial resources will follow. People selling a particular future need a way to get people to stop what they are doing and follow a new gold rush. The economist Carlota Perez has argued that hype is an inescapable feature of technological change. A 'gilded age' in which bubbles inflate and burst, inequality grows and new platforms are built can be followed by a 'golden age' during which meaningful technologies are deployed, benefitting the masses (Perez 2010). For AI, if we are to see a future golden age, the claims being made in the current gold rush must be scrutinised.

'REPEAT IT UNTIL IT IS TRUE'

In a 2017 paper on 'blind faith in data-driven technologies', social scientists Madeleine Clare Elish and danah boyd quote a data scientist who, like others working on AI, is ambivalent about the excitement that swirls around the science:

> I found that the people who ascribe the most power to statistics and data are not people who do statistics and data science. They are executives who give the vision talks about the power of data. ... I've seen so many cringe-inducing assertions ... In my head, I'm listening to all these things and am like, I remember that conversation, and the data on which that is based is so utterly flawed and unlikely to be true. But it supports the mythos... So let's

just repeat it until it is true. (Jeff Hammerbacher, quoted in Elish and boyd [2018])

AI has always been ripe for hype. Despite decades of research and development, the flabbiness of its definition and the flexibility of its aims make it, according to Enrico Coiera (2018), 'a Rorschach blot upon which many transfer their technological dreams or anxieties.' Some of the people working on AI and data science may be acutely aware of the uncertainties, which only become apparent up close. The people one or two steps removed may be more credulous. In 1958, when Frank Rosenblatt designed the Perceptron, an early neural network computer that could recognise a picture of a triangle, the *New York Times* reported that the military, who funded Rosenblatt's research, expected a future iteration to be 'able to walk, talk, see, write, reproduce itself and be conscious of its existence.'[5] Such hype is not harmless, nor are the scientists themselves blameless.

From the 1950s onwards, people at the heart of AI have found it hard to contain their excitement. Leading researchers like Alan Turing, Marvin Minsky and John McCarthy talked up the capabilities of computers while belittling human qualities. Scientists spoke about how thermostats, with superhuman powers of temperature control, 'think', while human brains were no more than 'meat machines.'[6] The 1970s and 80s saw bitter 'AI winters', when overexcitement about AI led to dashed expectations and a backlash from policymakers. In the UK, a 1973 report on AI from the mathematician Sir James Lighthill for the Science Research Council gave a rare and scathing account of a discipline's failure to live up to its own 'grandiose aims'.[7] Government support for AI research in both the UK and US was cut. Another boom followed as AI researchers focussed on specific problems rather than general intelligence, but again the expectations could not be matched by performance.

Now, AI has been reincarnated in the form of 'deep learning', enabled not by advances in scientific understanding of intelligence, but by an abundance of computing power and vast amounts of data extracted from the digitisation of everyday life. The possibilities are experienced by every user of Siri, Alexa and Google Translate and hidden in the infrastructures behind Amazon, Facebook and other platforms. Giant leaps in image recognition mean that computers can now 'see' parts of the analogue world without having to follow digital instructions. It is these achievements that have led many to conclude that the previously impossible prospect of a fully self-driving car is only a few years away.

With machine learning, particular technical achievements have been extrapolated into an imagined industrial revolution. Stories abound of computers outcompeting humans in acing medical qualifying exams, detecting breast cancers on X-rays, reading road signs and playing games like Chess, Go and Jeopardy.[8] A new generation of AI developers are finding their voices and amplifying past promises. Andrew Ng, the founder of the Google Brain AI team, wrote in 2016 that 'If a typical person can do a mental task with less than one second of thought, we can probably automate it using AI either now or in the near future.'[9] In a moment of peculiar irony, one Hong Kong venture capitalist claimed that the appointment of an algorithm to his board had protected the company from 'overhyped projects'.[10] A Finnish software company, Tieto, modestly claimed that 'our homegrown AI 'Alicia T' is a member of the leadership team, but not the chairman of the board'.[11]

An analysis of tech companies' earnings calls found that, following previous increases and decreases in hype around cloud computing and big data, 'artificial intelligence' was mentioned 16 times in 2014, 83 times in 2015, 399 times in 2016 and 1060 times in 2017.[12] A survey of European start-ups that brand themselves as 'AI' found that as many as 40% of them do not make use of any AI.[13] The suspicion is that a lot of what calls itself 'AI' may be a form of Mechanical Turk—old technology masquerading as new. As hype builds within industry, there is evidence that industry is also shaping the public debate. An analysis of recent media interest in AI from the Oxford Reuters Institute has found that most of the coverage follows announcements from the private sector. 12% of all articles referred to Elon Musk (Brennan et al. 2018).

A symptom of the dominance of the AI debate by corporations is that, alongside optimistic views of the benefits of AI, discussion of the downsides does not engage with many of the questions of inequality discussed in the previous chapter. Instead, it is skewed towards the apocalyptic. This pattern is not unique to AI. In 2000, the founder of Sun Microsystems Bill Joy wrote an infamous article in Wired magazine on 'Why the future doesn't need us'. Joy was persuaded into action by the hype that surrounded what was then the Next Big Thing—nanotechnology. His article reads like the product of a fever dream. His logic was that new technologies offer limitless power, which means they will inevitably bring about what he calls 'knowledge-enabled mass destruction':

> Failing to understand the consequences of our inventions while we are in the
> rapture of discovery and innovation seems to be a common fault of scientists
> and technologists; we have long been driven by the overarching desire to
> know that is the nature of science's quest, not stopping to notice that the
> progress to newer and more powerful technologies can take on a life of its
> own. (Joy 2000)

The article was interpreted by some technological optimists as a betrayal.
Others saw it as a leading light taking some responsibility for the pitfalls
of innovation. But, as is the case with today's powerful tech companies,
Joy had almost no sense that things could be different. One response a few
days after the article identified the problem:

> [Joy's] article describes a technological juggernaut thundering toward soci-
> ety... Joy can see the juggernaut clearly. What he can't see – which is precisely
> what makes his vision so scary – are any controls. (Seely Brown and Duguid
> 2000)

There is a tendency with technology to imagine its downsides in terms of
'risk', and to conclude that, because technologies are increasingly global,
we are all in it together. As I described in the previous chapter, the effects of
technology are always uneven. Elon Musk and Bill Joy have different wor-
ries from other people. As Kate Crawford (2016) has observed, there is a
reason why rich, white, powerful people imagine that the end of the world
or a robot takeover are the AI issues that should be given priority: these
would be the only things to challenge the dominance of that group. For
everyone else, there are more immediate concerns, such as the discriminatory use of algorithmic systems or the automation of labour. Technological
determinism has such a powerful hold on the imagination that, to twist a
quotation from the Marxist theorist Fredric Jamieson, it is easier for those
in power to imagine the end of the world than the governance of innovation.[14]

Crawford concluded in a later lecture that AI is, as other technologies
have been, 'plagued with a sense of technical inevitability' that limits the
imagination of both positive and negative possibilities.[15] For self-driving
cars, one of the most prominent topics for 'ethical' debate has been an
extension of the so-called 'trolley problem'. The scenario is that a robot
car is forced to make a choice in which one or many humans will die and
the question is how it should make its choice (e.g. Awad et al. 2018).
Such a dilemma is largely irrelevant for either engineering or policymaking.

We should remember that the trolley problem is a thought experiment, developed in the context of medical ethics, not a design challenge. Self-driving cars will never be omniscient. When outcomes are uncertain, the sensible failure mode is likely to involve minimising harm by braking hard rather than weighing up human lives. But, for technology boosters, trolley problems provide a convenient distraction from a real debate about the limits of technologies and the responsibilities of engineers.

At its most narrow, 'ethics' risks being framed by powerful actors in terms that amount to a form of moral blackmail. Again, the pattern is familiar from previous technologies. Philip Bond, then US Under-Secretary of Commerce for Technology said in 2004, 'Given nanotechnology's extraordinary economic and societal potential, it would be unethical, in my view, to attempt to halt scientific and technological progress in nanotechnology' (quoted in Swierstra and Rip 2007). A recent popular book on self-driving cars repeats a version of an argument used by Elon Musk in support of urgent self-driving car deployment: 'Delaying things by a single day basically entail[s] killing somewhere on earth an additional 3,000 people' (Burns and Shulgan 2018, p. 252).

THE DREAM OF AUTONOMY

If people think that AI is like human intelligence, they are less likely to worry about accountability: our existing rules will surely be able to sort things out. But the truth is that AI is very different. The engineers behind Google Translate admit that the extraordinary power of their tool comes not from mimicking a human interpreter but from the 'Unreasonable Effectiveness of Data' (Halevy et al. 2009). Using trillions of digitised words published in different languages, the software predicts likely translations, occasionally tweaked by helpful humans, to provide a constantly improving system. It is using brute force to approach the challenge of translation in a new way. The machine does not understand the language. If we asked it to explain itself, the answers would not satisfy a professional interpreter. This lack of accountability might be frustrating when we wonder why our emails get labelled as spam by AI filters. It matters more when Google Translate amplifies sexism as it switches to and from languages with gender neutral pronouns (Prates et al. 2018).

When algorithms are driving cars, the stakes are even higher. A self-driving car will never drive like a human. If we expect that it will, we will end up making bad decisions about the development of the technology.

When a self-driving car is involved in a crash, conventional ways of learning from car crashes will not be much help. It is hard to extract adequate explanations from machine learning systems. The creators of algorithms may not want to reveal trade secrets, they might not see the need for accountability, or they might justifiably claim that full interpretability of a deep neural network is impossible. The designers of neural networks are not clear, for example, how their algorithms know that a dog is a dog and a tree is a tree, although early research suggests that the machines and humans analyse images in very different ways, which opens up the possibility that a self-driving car's software could become confused either by mistake or malice and we wouldn't know why. The first fatal crashes involving software-driven cars have already revealed how complicated accountability will be (Stilgoe 2018).

The simple story about self-driving cars is that they merely replace a human driver with a software driver, doing the same job, but better. We should be sceptical not just of what we are being told, but also of what has been left out. Elon Musk's claims about the driving skills of his cars come with some conditions. In 2019, he reset his hype, saying that his cars' Autopilot system will be

> feature complete for full self-driving, this year, with certainty. This is something that we control, and I manage autopilot engineering directly, every week, in detail. So I'm certain of this. Then, when will regulators allow us even to have these features turned on?… these are externalities we don't quite control. And the conservatism of regulators varies a lot from one jurisdiction to another. My guess as to when we would think it's safe for somebody to essentially fall asleep and wake up at their destination? Probably towards the end of next year… I don't know when will regulators will agree.[16]

Musk is claiming that the hardware of the technology is complete, waiting just around the corner but held back by two things. One is the recalcitrance of regulators (although it is not clear which rules are in the way). The other is the AI software that would replace the driver.

Software is a convenient medium for the imagination of futures, because it seems detached from the inertia of the material world. If innovation is just about software, the story goes that it can accelerate without limit. According to the evangelists, innovation is governed by Moore's Law, which states that computer power increases exponentially over time. But Moore's law is not a law and it certainly doesn't apply to all technologies. Moore's law is actually a set of targets for the running of a race. As with the space race, it is a strategy for the reinforcement of a set of imagined needs. The 'law' has historically been a self-fulfilling prophecy, thanks to massive investment and coordination across the microchip industry (Mody 2016). After decades of remarkable target-hitting, it is now proving impossible to match despite increasing investment. Meanwhile, some areas of technological change, such as nuclear energy and drug development, are getting slower and more expensive (Scannell et al. 2012).

Seeing self-driving as a question of software has tempted companies like Uber, Tesla and Waymo to release products onto the streets only months after beginning research on them. Software is a big 'if', but Elon Musk portrays it as small. His dream of instant autonomy promises to change the world without changing the world. It suggests that self-driving cars will just plug-and-play. It overlooks all of the other parts of the systems that make technologies work. For cars to function, we need infrastructure, laws, social norms, driver education and more besides. All of these would need to be augmented to suit self-driving cars, with the addition of detailed digital maps and connectivity between vehicles. This will take time, and the changes could be bitterly contested, much to the frustration of those in the vanguard of innovation. One reason why innovators' technological predictions are often so wrong is that so much of what needs to happen is beyond their control: technological change requires social change. Musk, however, is less interested in the accuracy of his predictions than in their persuasive power. Because of their imagined future capabilities, Musk has referred to his company's cars as 'an appreciating asset'. And the evidence is that it works. Tens of thousands of Tesla customers have paid thousands of dollars for 'Full self-driving' even though the technology doesn't work yet. In 2019, a survey reported that 40% of drivers thought that a Tesla was already self-driving.[17]

The unglamorous business of infrastructure, policymaking and social change gets less attention than apparently frictionless improvements in software, but is more important if the public benefits of new technologies are to be realised. Carlota Perez (2010) argues that the installation of new technologies that happens during disruptive 'gilded ages' to be followed by decades of difficult development work in order to ensure that the 'golden age' benefits follow. Dan Sarewitz and Brad Allenby (2011) refer to cars, mobile phones and computer programmes as Level 1 technologies. They call roads, petrol stations, highway patrols, mobile phone networks and the hardware of the Internet Level 2 technologies. We need both, but Level 1 gets more attention. The stories we tell about past techno-logical change emphasise the revolutionary rather than the incremental. Innovators are incentivised to adopt a 'fake it till you make it' approach. The novelties are emphasised to the point at which the promises of new technology become demands (Van Lente 2000).

In the US, there is evidence that hope of self-driving transport being just around the corner is putting pressure on already-fragile proposals for public transport. In 2017, Nashville voters took against one light rail and bus scheme following a campaign by libertarians and tech enthusiasts. One Nashville Council member, Robert Swope, was quoted as saying some months before the key vote:

> In 15 years, no one will own a car anymore... I can show you places around this world I have been to where Level 5 autonomous vehicles are in operation today... Why are we not embracing this?[18]

'Level 5' refers to a self-driving car that can operate autonomously in any circumstances. They do not exist and, if we take the definition literally, never will. Nevertheless, Swope advocated 'autonomous vehicle systems that will replace the need for large, costly mass transportation' with little considera-tion of what else would be required.[19] In Florida, Republican state senator Jeff Brandes has attacked long-term transport planning in general, as well as particular public transit schemes, claiming that self-driving cars will make buses and trains obsolete in a matter of years. He has said repeatedly, 'It's like they're designing the pony express in the world of the telegraph.'[20]

Hype and the Responsibilities of Scientists

For an indication of the role of hype in science, and the risks that it brings, we can look to the Human Brain Project. Following the model of the much-hyped Human Genome Project at the turn of the Millennium, the Euro-pean Union promised a billion Euros to neuroscience research, with the expectation that this would also boost European industry. Henry Markram, the project's leading light, claimed in a 2009 TED talk, 'it is not impossible to build a brain. We can do it within 10 years and, if we do succeed, we will send to TED, in 10 years, a hologram to talk to you.'[21] Needless to say, the project has been unable to live up to its hype. Ten years on, the promises of scientific breakthroughs and industrial revolutions look empty. Soon after the project began, it was riven by infighting. Christoph Ebell, who took over the project's leadership after 800 neuroscientists signed an open letter attacking Markram's vision, lamented the hype around neuroscience: 'you start promising more, and everyone starts repeating it, even the scientists. It's a feedback loop. And with so much money at stake, the feedback loop is very effective'.[22]

Scientists in universities face growing pressure to attract research funding and push their work towards greater social relevance. In such an environment, it is hard to resist the urge to accentuate the positive, over-promise in research proposals and over-claim in scientific papers. Scientists' expertise is arcane and research is highly specialised, so it can make sense to organise by bandwagons. Hype is a signal that can be communicated beyond the cognoscenti. Funding for the Human Genome Project or the War on Cancer would not have come without hyping the possibility of curing disease. Neither effort delivered on their promises, but both redirected money towards researchers and contributed to substantial medical advances.

Nevertheless, scientists can often feel torn. They must compete for attention, knowing that this attention can raise false hope and distort research agendas. Once bandwagons are built, they need to be kept full and moving. An individual scientist may come to personify an area of scientific excitement, which can encourage dishonesty and even fraud. The Korean stem cell scientist Hwang Woo-suk was once a national icon and international celebrity for his work in embryo cloning. After he was found to have conducted fraudulent and unethical research, he told a journalist, 'I created an illusion and made it look as if it were real... I was drunk in the bubble I created'.[23]

Hype is a symptom of the conflicted role that science plays in society. Science is expected to deliver truth, but it is also expected to deliver progress. And while on matters of fact scientists may protect their evidence jealously, holding onto rationality and responsibility in a discussion about the future is far harder. As the avant-garde artist Naum Gabo (1920) wrote in his 'Realistic Manifesto' a century ago, 'Not to lie about the future is impossible and one can lie about it at will.' Much of the time, hype has few consequences. Helga Nowotny (2010) calls it a 'risk-free mortgage on the future'. Even following a string of broken promises and dashed expectations, it is possible for scientists to argue that this time it will be different.

Scientists inside a bubble may benefit from resources and attention, but they may also feel trapped. There are examples of scientists using their proximity to prick the bubbles that are close to them or even surrounding them.[24] But in most cases the dynamic is that the people inside the bubble are able to blame everyone else for its inflation. The problem is a collective one, like traffic: drivers complain when they are in it, even though they are it.

This is not to say that scientists should stop speculating. If societies are to anticipate and make decisions about the possibilities of new technologies, scientists' prognostications are vital. The people at the frontiers of research are most likely to know the limits of technology. Scientists' insights should, however, be taken as the start rather than the end of the conversation. The trouble is that speculation is often asymmetrical. Scientists involved in innovation are incentivised to talk up the positive possibilities and suppress the negative ones. Science should, in the words of US Physicist Harvey Brooks (1994), act as 'the conscience of technology', but scientists in areas like AI that are benefitting from governmental and corporate largesse may find it hard to swim against the tide.

As self-driving cars have met the real world, some of the expectations have come down to earth. In 2018, a number of companies developing the technology were quoted explaining how self-driving cars were harder than they thought they would be. But this is mostly because companies were choosing not to think very hard about the difficulties. Some companies have been quietly critical of Tesla's system lulling users into a false sense of autonomy. But some of the most notable critics are those closest to the research, who have kept a watchful eye and are unsurprised. Gary Marcus, a university professor whose company was bought by Uber, has been critical of self-driving car enthusiasts who, having hyped the technology, are now 'redefining the goalposts to make the job easier'.[25] Dean Pomerleau, who conducted self-driving car experiments in the 90s, has taken aim at Tesla's hype:

> Claiming its vehicles will soon be 'feature complete' for full self-driving is one more step in the unconscionable practices that Tesla is already engaged in with Autopilot — overselling its capabilities and reliability when marketing its vehicles and then blaming the driver for not reading the manual and paying constant attention when the technology inevitably fails.[26]

More stridently, there is Zachary Lipton, a colleague of Pomerleau's in machine learning at Carnegie Mellon University, who has ventured well outside the lab to counter what he sees as misinformation flowing from journalists and tech developers, but calls his efforts 'just a pebble in the rapids of crap'.[27] The voices of critical scientists are vital to the responsible development of technology. Unfortunately, they are often drowned out. It is often said that governments are bad at thinking about the future. It is true that electoral cycles incentivise short-termism. But governments have also abdicated their responsibility to assess the futures that are being imagined in the present day and hold them to account. Hype is a way of deliberately concealing the politics of technology and privatising progress. If we overinvest our hopes in new technologies, we underinvest in other necessary but less glamorous areas, including education, public health, infrastructure and maintenance. We should therefore look for a more collaborative alternative.

NOTES

1. What will the future look like? Elon Musk speaks at TED2017, TED Blog, 28 April 2017, https://blog.ted.com/what-will-the-future-look-like-elon-musk-speaks-at-ted2017/.
2. Interviewed on CBS 60 minutes, 9 December 2018, https://www.cbsnews.com/video/elon-musk-screen-time-ryan-speedo-green/.
3. The quote is taken from 'What can Elon Musk's personal flight records tell of Tesla's 'ominous' year?' *Washington Post*, 29 January 2019.
4. Arendt (1958) quoted in B. Adam and C. Groves (2007).
5. New navy device learns by doing; Psychologist shows embryo of computer designed to read and grow wiser, *New York Times*, 8 July 1958.
6. The thermostat example is used by John McCarthy (1983). The meat machine comment comes from Marvin Minsky. Luke Muelhauser's study of past AI forecasts is a useful analysis of AI early AI hype. What should we learn from past AI forecasts?, Open Philanthropy project, 2016, https://www.openphilanthropy.org/focus/global-catastrophic-risks/potential-risks-advanced-artificial-intelligence/what-should-we-learn-past-ai-forecasts.
7. 'Artificial intelligence: A general survey', Professor Sir James Lighthill, FRS, in Artificial Intelligence: a paper symposium, Science Research Council 1973.
8. These examples and more are provided by Jamie Susskind (2018).
9. What artificial intelligence can and can't do right now, *Harvard Business Review*, 9 November 2016, https://hbr.org/2016/11/what-artificial-intelligence-can-and-cant-do-right-now.
10. Artificial intelligence gets a seat in the boardroom Hong Kong venture capitalist sees AI running Asian companies within 5 years. Nikkei Asian Review, May 10, 2017 https://asia.nikkei.com/Business/Artificial-intelligence-gets-a-seat-in-the-boardroom.

11. In a smarter society, AI will manage but it's humans who will lead. Tieto talks blog, 18 February 2018, https://perspectives.tieto.com/blog/2018/02/in-a-smarter-society-ai-will-manage-but-its-humans-who-will-lead/.
12. The AI Index 2018 Annual Report, AI Index Steering Committee, Human-Centered AI Initiative, Stanford University, Stanford, CA, December 2018, http://cdn.aiindex.org/2018/AI%20Index%202018%20Annual%20Report.pdf.
13. MMC, The state of AI 2019 report, https://www.mmcventures.com/wp-content/uploads/2019/02/The-State-of-AI-2019-Divergence.pdf.
14. Jameson's statement was that 'it has become easier to imagine the end of the world than the end of capitalism'.
15. From a lecture, 'Just an engineer: The politics of AI' at the Royal Society in London, 17 July 2018. https://www.youtube.com/watch?v=HPopJb5aDyA.
16. On the road to full autonomy with Elon Musk, ARK Invest podcast, 19 February 2019, https://ark-invest.com/research/podcast/elon-musk-podcast.
17. From a survey by Thatcham Research, Euro NCAP and Global NCAP, https://www.thatcham.org/automated-driving-hype-is-dangerously-confusing-drivers-study-reveals/. This expectation has created new risks, and likely been a factor in the deaths of at least two Tesla drivers (see Stilgoe 2018).
18. The lurking question on Nashville's transit plan: What about self-driving cars?, *Tennessean*, 23 October 2017. https://eu.tennessean.com/story/news/2017/10/23/lurking-question-nashvilles-transit-plan-what-self-driving-cars/776070001/.
19. Self-driving cars will not be Nashville's transit savior, *Tennessean*, 4 December 2019. https://eu.tennessean.com/story/opinion/2017/12/04/self-driving-cars-not-nashvilles-transit-savior/107502418/.
20. Trains and self-driving cars, headed for a (political) collision, *Fortune*, 3 November 2014, fortune.com/2014/11/02/trains-autonomous-vehicles-politics.
21. Henry Markram: A brain in a supercomputer, TED Talk, 20 October 2009.
22. Why the human brain project went wrong—And how to fix it, *Scientific American*, 1 October 2015. https://www.scientificamerican.com/article/why-the-human-brain-project-went-wrong-and-how-to-fix-it/.
23. Korean scientist's new project: Rebuild after cloning disgrace, *New York Times*, 28 February 2014, https://www.nytimes.com/2014/03/01/world/asia/scientists-new-project-rebuild-after-cloning-disgrace.html.
24. The historian Nathaniel Comfort refers to a compendium of hype around the Human Genome Project that was compiled by geneticist Jonathan Eisen. Why the hype around medical genetics is a public enemy, *Aeon Magazine*, https://aeon.co/ideas/why-the-hype-around-medical-genetics-is-a-public-enemy.

25. To get ready for robot driving, some want to reprogram pedestrians, Bloomberg News, 16 August 2018, https://www.bloomberg.com/ news/articles/2018-08-16/to-get-ready-for-robot-driving-some-want-to-reprogram-pedestrians.
26. Quoted in 'Tesla's promise of "full-self-driving" angers autonomous vehicle experts', Matt McFarland, CNN Business, 2 March 2019, https://edition. cnn.com/2019/03/02/tech/tesla-full-self-driving/index.html.
27. Quoted in '"The discourse is unhinged": How the media gets AI alarmingly wrong', The Guardian, 25 July 2018. https://www.theguardian. com/technology/2018/jul/25/ai-artificial-intelligence-social-media-bots-wrong.

References

Adam, B., & Groves, C. (2007). *Future matters: Action, knowledge, ethics*. Leiden: Brill.

Allenby, B. R., & Sarewitz, D. (2011). *The techno-human condition*. Cambridge: MIT press.

Arendt, H. (1958/1998). *The human condition*. Chicago: University of Chicago Press.

Awad, E., Dsouza, S., Kim, R., Schulz, J., Henrich, J., Shariff, A., et al. (2018). The moral machine experiment. *Nature, 563*(7729), 7759.

Barbrook, R., & Cameron, A. (1996). The californian ideolgy. *Science as Culture, 6*(1), 44–72.

Borup, M., Brown, N., Konrad, K., & Van Lente, H. (2006). The sociology of expectations in science and technology. *Technology Analysis & Strategic Management, 18*(3–4), 285–298.

Brennan, J. S., Howard, P. N., & Kleis Nielsen, R. (2018). *An industry-led debate: How UK media cover artificial intelligence*. Reuters Institute for the Study of Journalism. https://reutersinstitute.politics.ox.ac.uk/sites/default/ files/2018-12/Brennen_UK_Media_Coverage_of_AI_FINAL.pdf.

Brooks, H. (1994). The relationship between science and technology. *Research Policy, 23*(5), 477–486.

Burns, L., & Shulgan, C. (2018). *Autonomy: The quest to build the driverless car and how it will reshape our world* (p. 252). London: HarperCollins.

Coiera, E. (2018). The fate of medicine in the time of AI. *Lancet, 392*(10162), 2331–2332.

Crawford, K. (2016, June 25). Artificial intelligence's white guy problem. *New York Times*.

Elish, M. C., & boyd, d. (2018). Situating methods in the magic of Big Data and AI. *Communication Monographs, 85*(1), 57–80.

Gabo, N., & Pevsner, A. (1920). The realistic manifesto. *Russian Art of the Avant-Garde Theory and Criticism 1902, 34*, 209–214.

Halevy, A., Norvig, P., & Pereira, F. (2009). The unreasonable effectiveness of data. *IEEE Intelligent Systems*, 24(2), 8–12.

Joy, B. (2000, April 1). Why the future doesn't need us. *Wired Magazine*. https://www.wired.com/2000/04/joy-2/.

McCarthy, J. (1983). The little thoughts of thinking machines. *Psychology Today*, *17*(12), 46–49.

Mody, C. C. (2016). *The long arm of Moore's law: Microelectronics and American science*. Cambridge: MIT Press.

Nowotny, H. (2010). *Insatiable curiosity: Innovation in a fragile future*. Cambridge: MIT Press.

Perez, C. (2010, June). *The advance of technology and major bubble collapses: Historical regularities and lessons for today*. Paper for the Engelsberg Seminar on 'The Future of Capitalism', Ax:son Foundation, Sweden. http://www.carlotaperez.org/downloads/media/PEREZTechnologyandbubblesforEngelsbergseminar.pdf.

Pollock, N., & Williams, R. (2016). *How industry analysts shape the digital future*. Oxford: Oxford University Press.

Prates, M. O., Avelar, P. H., & Lamb, L. (2018). *Assessing gender bias in machine translation—A case study with Google translate*. arXiv preprint arXiv:1809.02208.

Scannell, J. W., Blanckley, A., Boldon, H., & Warrington, B. (2012). Diagnosing the decline in pharmaceutical R&D efficiency. *Nature Reviews Drug Discovery*, *11*(3), 191.

Seely Brown, J., & Paul D. (2000, April 13). *A response to Bill Joy and the doom-and-gloom technofuturists*. The Industry Standard. http://engl102-f12-lombardy.wikispaces.umb.edu/file/view/A+Response+to+Bill+Joy+and+the+Doom+and+Gloom+Technofuturists+by+John+Seely+Brown+and+Paul+Duguid.pdf.

Stilgoe, J. (2018). Machine learning, social learning and the governance of self-driving cars. *Social Studies of Science*, 48(1), 25–56.

Susskind, J. (2018). *Future politics: Living together in a world transformed by tech*. Oxford: Oxford University Press.

Swierstra, T., & Rip, A. (2007). Nano-ethics as NEST-ethics: Patterns of moral argumentation about new and emerging science and technology. *Nanoethics*, *1*(1), 3–20.

Van Lente, H. (2000). Forceful futures: From promise to requirement. In N. Brown & B. Rappert (Eds.), *Contested futures: A sociology of prospective techno-science* (pp. 43–64). London: Routledge.

CHAPTER 5

The Collaborative State

Democratising Innovation

On an otherwise deserted university campus outside Milton Keynes, one Saturday before Christmas 2018, 30 people from various walks of British life gathered for an unusual conversation. Their task was to help British policymakers think about self-driving cars. This was their third meeting. At the previous one, the participants had been the first members of the public to try out one company's prototype vehicle. The experience had elicited mixed reviews. Most of the passengers were impressed, but aware that their experience was not the real deal. They wondered, understandably, how the car would behave without a test driver, away from the tightly-controlled conditions of a test track. Seeing the car up close brought the autonomous dream they had seen elsewhere down to earth.

The forum had been initiated by Sciencewise, a UK Government programme that has run public dialogue exercises for more than fifteen years. These members of the public, along with people in four other places around the UK, brought their experiences and perspectives to a discussion that would normally be regarded as too technical for public debate. Most saw clear potential in the technology, but they were concerned that the benefits—making transport safer; helping people with mobility problems—might not be realised if the technology was badly managed. Almost nobody bought the idea that a transition to a self-driving future would simply be a matter of letting computers take the wheel. Most thought that self-driving cars would need new infrastructure and that other road users would have to

© The Author(s) 2020
J. Stilgoe, *Who's Driving Innovation?*,
https://doi.org/10.1007/978-3-030-32320-2_5

behave differently around them. They were concerned not just about giving up control of their cars, but about losing control of their mobility. They felt that a self-driving future would provide less freedom, not more. Some of the comments gathered over the three days suggest a deep ambivalence:

> Cars were liberating for the workings classes and older people. This seems to be restricting choice.

> There will be risks, we will learn from accidents, but I don't want my family to be those on the back of which the learning happens.

> What if someone doesn't want a driverless car?

> It will be for the greater good, but it worries me. I don't know if I personally can make all the changes required to adapt to this world.

Towards the end of the third day, after more than fifteen hours of deliberation, it came time to tell the government what they thought. The participants had more questions than answers, but they were clear on some things. First, they were worried that the technology would just be a luxury and they wanted access for all. (Some of the participants from rural Wales were particularly concerned that the technology would only be developed in and for cities.) Second, they thought that the costs of implementing the technology should be borne by the people who were benefitting. Third, they wanted the development of the technology to be overseen by a range of people, not just engineers, businesses or civil servants.[1]

Historically, policymakers' approach to the regulation of technologies has been to wait and see—assess the risks, costs and benefits and respond if things go wrong. In this mode, the public are seen as a problem to be managed; they are assumed to be ignorant, recalcitrant or both. By seeing people as a source of wisdom, discussions such as those convened by Sciencewise point to a more collaborative form of governance.

Self-driving cars, and the places and lifestyles that are created around them, represent an open-ended social experiment whose participants will potentially include us all. It's an experiment that urgently needs to be democratised. Making the technology work means more than getting the AI right. It will require genuine collaboration—in the literal sense of experimenting together—between technology developers, governments, civil society and the public.

LEFT TO THEIR OWN DEVICES

Technological innovation is produced by the interplay of public and private sector institutions. And yet we have been led to believe that innovation happens despite rather than because of the public sector. If Silicon Valley can be said to have a philosophy, it is one of disruption, 'move fast and break things', in Mark Zuckerberg's words (now heard less often). The founding editor of Wired magazine, reflecting on his magazine's principles, noted how, 15 years after the magazine's creation, 'Governments are still here, presumptuous and bossy as ever.'[2] In the disruptive worldview, government is a barrier to innovation and deregulation is a religion.

The assumption is that, if only companies could cast off the shackles of government, the benefits would flow freely. Some Silicon Valley leaders, inspired by Ayn Rand, have even advocated 'seasteading', the building of floating start-up communities that are untethered from the rules of nation states. Peter Thiel thinks we are in 'a deadly race between politics and technology' and wants 'an open frontier for experimenting with new ideas for government'. Larry Page would like to 'set aside some small part of the world' for unregulated experimentation.[3] Some innovators are captivated by the possibility of escape: escape from regulation; escape from the constraints of human bodies or planet earth; escape from transport systems designed to inclusively accommodate others.

The idea of disruptive innovation began as a description rather than a prescription. The aim was to explain how well-established firms with technologies that were firmly entrenched could be undone by upstarts selling apparently inferior alternatives. The business school professor Clayton Christensen (1997) repackaged ideas from Joseph Schumpeter to explain the demise of mainframe computers and department stores. We might now add video rental, analogue photography, bricks-and-mortar bookshops and print journalism to the litany. Writing in the *New Yorker*, Jill Lepore (2014) argues that the theory doesn't work either as description or prediction, but that this is not the point. Disruption functions as a credo for our age, in which old ideas of 'progress', now seen as naively utopian, are supplanted by new ones of 'innovation', with little questioning of the purpose.

The irony of disruption is that, while claiming to be radical, it is atavistic and devoid of the imagination or creativity of Schumpeter's 'creative destruction' (Lepore 2014). Some of the assumptions behind the development of AI suggest a peculiar conservatism. The reliance on swathes of historical data reiterates and exacerbates historical bias. The change offered by disruptive innovation tends to be more of the same: more hype and growing inequalities. Left to their own devices, experiments in disruption can become the new normal. So how can governments put themselves back into the development of technologies?

'BOLD, PERSISTENT EXPERIMENTATION'

For self-driving cars, we can quickly see the limits of a model based on disruptive innovation. Self-driving cars will never be as autonomous as their salespeople would like us to believe. For cars to be self-driving, they will need to communicate with one another and their environment, they will need the world to be machine-readable and they will need other road users to adjust their behaviour. If self-driving cars are to increase social mobility, governments will need to invest in infrastructure. Otherwise, the technology will just go where the money is and widen inequalities.

Since the New Deal's 'bold, persistent experimentation' in the first half of the twentieth century and the arms and space races of the second half, Western governments have lost confidence in their ability to invest in and shape new technologies. Over the twentieth century, the public sector was often, as Mariana Mazzucato (2015) has argued, vitally entrepreneurial, taking experimental risks that companies could never stomach and laying the groundwork for transformative technologies. (The US Government's Defense Advanced Projects Research Agency built the platform that became the Internet, funded the development of Siri and later staged competitions that boosted the development of self-driving cars.) But as tech companies have become more self-assured, governments have become neurotic. Dirigisme has fallen out of fashion as policymakers focus more on market failure than public value.

If big ideas for social and technological improvement like the US 'Green New Deal' are to take flight, governments will have to recover their appetite for imagination and experimentation. Seeing public policy as a form of grand experiment is a tradition with roots in the thinking of pragmatists like John Dewey. This approach, rather than clinging to the false certainties of cost-benefit analysis or fixed ideas of right and wrong, sees values as hypotheses to be tested in the real world. Pragmatists are sceptical of utopianism and more interested in how we can know where we are going, keep our options open and change direction if needs be. The hope is that progress can be democratised, inviting citizens into a discussion of a desirable shared future.

More recently, the enthusiasm for experimentation has been taken up in areas like international development and education policy. A more scientific approach to finding out what works has included the use of randomised control trials, more normally used to test medical treatments. More than a third of UK schools have now taken part in RCTs.[4] In areas of potentially explosive innovation, the blast can be contained by regulators allowing a degree of controlled experimentation. The British Financial Conduct Authority, formed after the 2007/2008 financial crisis, has joined other financial regulators in running 'regulatory sandboxes' in which new financial products can be tested with real consumers but protecting others from any fallout.[5] In the US, there is an established pattern in which states act as what Supreme Court Judge Louis Brandeis called 'laboratories for democracy', trying out new policies before nationwide implementation. In recent years, some of the world's more assertive cities have begun to regard themselves as testbeds for the nurturing of tomorrow's 'smart cities', not just dripping with tech but also engaged in a process on ongoing data-gathering and learning.

Enthusiasts for a more experimental state may feel as though their initiatives and the learning generated by them are being held back by a mixture of political conservatism and bureaucratic inertia. However, the politics of experimentation are inescapable and need to be watched carefully. Values can never just be evaluated scientifically. It matters who is in charge of the experiment. Experiments in public are also experiments on the public. Even well-intentioned experimentation in education or welfare reform can be destablising for people who may be among society's most vulnerable. Herbert Marcuse's (1968) analysis, that 'To experiment and play with the apparatus is at present the monopoly of those who work for the preservation and expansion of the status quo' remains true. The infrastructure of our online lives, while it may feel static, is in fact a set of perpetual experiments. Google and Facebook conduct 'A/B testing' in which groups of users are watched to see how they respond to tweaked versions of services. This form of testing is intentionally directionless. Evan Spiegel, the creator of Snapchat, has argued that this form of thoughtless measurement can be toxic: 'I think you can end up in a place that you don't even understand because you A/B-tested your way there'.[6]

In Toronto, Sidewalk Labs, a Google sister company, are building a 'Living Lab'. Canadian Prime Minister Justin Trudeau hailed 'A world leader in urban innovation. Sidewalk Labs will create a testbed for new technologies... that will help us build smarter, greener, more inclusive cities'. But some citizens felt like lab rats rather than scientists. In what Google called the 'world's first neighborhood built from the internet up,' the immediate concern was one of data privacy, but under the surface, questions swirled about who would end up paying and who was really benefiting from the grand plan.[7] In 'smart cities', the question rears its head: who is experimenting upon whom?

HEALTHY INNOVATION

There are areas in which the public sector has resisted getting pushed around by the promise of new technologies and tried with some success to pull technologies to its own ends. For most countries, the clearest example is defence, where governments are happy to tell companies what is needed. In some countries, transport systems have been collaboratively designed to meet social goals, even if disagreements about public/private partnerships never evaporate. For the UK, the collaborative state is best exemplified by the National Health Service. Here, there is close attention to the purposes, processes and products of innovation and careful experimentation. In healthcare, the stakes are high. If people's lives are in the balance, their rights are jeopardised if they participate in trials of new treatments, and the relationship between a technology and its users depends upon high levels of trust, the case for governance is clear. But the model has important lessons for other areas.

The first lesson is that health technologies are rigorously assessed by independent bodies. New drugs are evaluated not just in terms of whether they are safe, but also for their benefits. When science creates new possibilities in, for example, fertility, genetic sequencing or even genome editing, these are explored not just by medics but from a range of perspectives. Organisations like the Human Fertilisation and Embryology Authority bring in insights from ethics, the social sciences, medicine, basic science and, increasingly, the general public.

The second lesson is that hype is kept in check. The NHS recognises that claims made about new technologies can distort as well as inform. In the UK, private companies are banned from advertising prescription medicines directly to consumers. Most claims about the benefits of treatments are filtered through doctors, who are professionally obliged to help patients make sense of the promises of new treatments. Clearly, as sources of information proliferate, this form of control becomes harder, but the system makes it hard to sell snake oil.

The third lesson is that inequalities are seen as a problem to be tackled. It helps that the National Health Service is guided by the principle of universal healthcare. In practice, the NHS works to reduce health inequalities, even if this comes at a cost of less benefit for the richest and healthiest people. Other countries may not agree with such a settlement, but the point is that the NHS recognises healthcare as unavoidably political. There are choices to be made with scarce resources. As with other areas of policymaking, health professionals still struggle to justify investment in infrastructure, prevention and monitoring, even though these are usually more cost effective in the long run.

Finally, experimentation in healthcare is carefully organised. There is an awareness that new approaches and new medicines could have losers as well as winners and risks as well as benefits. A system of clinical trials allows for the controlled testing of powerful, potentially dangerous technologies. At the same time, there is recognition that not all technologies can be assessed in advance of their release, so there are systems for the trialling and monitoring of innovations that may be beneficial.

The NHS's collaborative state is far from perfect. Some would say it is too cautious in giving patients, particularly those with few options left, access to new technologies. Others would point to recent controversies surrounding patient data and AI and say that the NHS still has not worked out how to deal with technologies outside its comfort zone. Patients with rare or chronic diseases may feel that the system is still too paternalistic; they would like to be more involved and have their own expertise recognised. That said, the NHS has built up a capacity to deal with and steer new technologies that few other organisations can rival. This is not to say that it should just be emulated in other sectors—the investments and expertise required are huge—but it is a striking alternative to a laissez-faire model of innovation.

With artificial intelligence, for governments and citizens to become collaborators, rather than just leaseholders on laboratories or regulators of others' experiments, they need to rebuild their capacity to make sense of technological possibilities. In this book, I have put forward the optimistic argument that AI could be redirected towards greater public value. There are no inevitable technologies of AI, and there are important choices ahead. At the moment, the signs do not bode well. AI is likely to lead to a concentration of power for the small number of organisations—big tech firms or the Chinese government—who control data. High-stakes decisions may be taken in ways that make accountability and transparency hard. Policy-makers in most countries are fixated on competing in an AI 'race', even though they have no sense of where they are heading. Where they ask difficult questions, these are often phrased in narrow terms of 'AI ethics'. Few people are asking who stands to benefit from AI. Policymakers need to ask what AI would look like if it were to benefit those who have lost out from past technologies. Currently, most of the important decisions are being devolved to scientists and technology developers rather than being discussed democratically. We should indeed demand from innovators more responsibility, more ethical reflection and more honesty about technological limits, but we should not pretend that self-regulation is the answer. As a high-profile test case for real-world AI, self-driving cars are an opportunity to improve upon innovation-as-usual.

Putting People Back in the Driving Seat

When the governor of Arizona invited Uber to use his state as a laboratory for their self-driving cars, getting little in return, he was happy to be disrupted. He saw innovation as an end in itself. The death of Elaine Herzberg revealed the risks and the limits of this approach. Uber's missteps are an early warning. The hope among US federal regulators is that there will be a market incentive for self-driving car safety, but the history of automobile safety suggests that companies won't go in that direction unless they are pushed (Vinsel 2019).

An alternative model is to be found in Silicon Valley itself. Even though California is home to a particular brand of technological libertarianism, its state government is more self-confident than most in the US, and its policymakers more able to assert themselves. A decade ago, the California Public Utilities Commission were taken by surprise with the arrival of companies like Uber that, claiming to be in the software business rather than the transport business, were given a free reign by regulators. For self-driving cars, the Commission have made some demands on an industry that is on the cusp of providing commercial services: they want companies to test for 90 days on public roads before rolling out, they want to see performance data from the tests and from any future services, and they want to be able to get voice recordings from inside cars. The tech developers aren't delighted by the approach. They would rather hold onto data, which could be the currency for self-driving innovation, and they would like the government to wait and see what the risks of the technology are rather than engage proactively.

California's approach, criticised by some as old-fashioned protectionism for incumbent transport providers, suggests the start of a new relationship between the public and private sectors. It turns an experiment into a collaboration. It helps ensure that, as technologies emerge and morph, some of the learning is shared. The focus is still narrow—ensuring that the testing of new technologies is reasonably safe—but it starts a more collaborative process of getting to grips with new technologies.

In Massachusetts, some lawmakers have additional concerns about self-driving cars. A proactive proposal from two state senators includes what they call a 'zombie tax' on cars that drive without any occupants, which would pollute and clog up streets just to avoid parking fees. As well as sharing data, they also want self-driving cars to be zero-emission and clearly labelled so that other road users can know what they are dealing with.

Policymakers should not just be clear on what they want from technology. They should also seek to understand and modulate the laws that are shaping technology. Prolific innovators like Thomas Edison understood the importance of intellectual property (until IBM came along, Edison held more patents than anyone) and technological standards (Edison knew that the contest between alternating current and direct current electricity was crucial, even though he eventually lost). For self-driving cars, the battle to define the rules of the game will be just as fierce as the approaches different companies take in trying to win it. Seemingly innocuous or technocratic discussions around, for example, the sharing of data or the timings of traffic lights could prove fateful. Given the potential for cartels of technological interest to form, policymakers need to pay close attention if they are to identify the important decision points before decisions get made by default.

For the social experiment of self-driving cars to become a collaboration, governments need to act now. They will need to ensure that there is social learning to accompany progress in machine learning. They will need to come up with rules for self-driving cars to follow. Otherwise, the risk is that tomorrow's rules of the road will be set by private experiments happening today. The history of the motor car tells us plenty about who benefits from certain forms of technology and how to avoid repeating past mistakes. We know how to avoid urban sprawl, congestion and pollution. New technologies provide an opportunity to act on this knowledge. Governments will need to be clear on the principles that self-driving technologies should work towards. If they want universal, or at least widespread, access to mobility, they need to pull technology to this end. Self-driving cars will be an important technology in their own right, but they are also an opportunity for policymakers to develop and demonstrate a new relationship between technology and society.

In the post-war twentieth century, technological optimism was accompanied by well-organised technology assessment. Governments in the UK, US and elsewhere who were funding new technologies also built institutions that were able to make sense of technological possibilities, challenge hype and maintain a focus on public benefit. The US Office of Technology Assessment, created in 1972 and killed by a Republican Congress in 1995, produced landmark analyses of genetic engineering, computer security, weapons in space and more. Equivalent bodies in the Netherlands, Denmark and elsewhere developed more democratic models, blending expert analysis and public deliberation. In the twenty-first century, technological progress has been privatised. Innovators may tell themselves that innovation is accelerating, but to many outsiders it looks directionless. The capacity for technology assessment has been allowed to atrophy—a victim of short-termism, free-market thinking and globalisation—when it is more needed than ever.

NOTES

1. The full report is available at https://assets.publishing.service.gov.uk/government/uploads/system/uploads/attachment_data/file/837958/cav-public-acceptability-dialogue-engagement-report.pdf.
2. In a letter to his kids, Wired's founding editor recalls the dawn of the digital revolution, *Wired Magazine*, 19 May 2008. https://www.wired.com/2008/05/ff-15th-rossetto/.
3. The first Thiel quote is from The Education of a Libertarian, Cato Unbound, 13 April 2009, https://www.cato-unbound.org/2009/04/13/peter-thiel/education-libertarian. The others are from 'Has Google gone gaga?', Bryan Appleyard, *The Sunday Times*, 3 June 2013.
4. England has become one of the world's biggest education laboratories, *The Economist*, 31 March 2018, https://www.economist.com/britain/2018/03/31/england-has-become-one-of-the-worlds-biggest-education-laboratories.
5. See Jenik and Lauer (2017).
6. Snap's chief Evan Spiegel: taming tech and fighting with Facebook, *The Financial Times*, 28 December 2018.

7. How smart should a city be? Toronto is finding out, City Lab, 7 September 2018, https://www.citylab.com/design/2018/09/how-smart-should-a-city-be-toronto-is-finding-out/569116/. See also Goodman and Powles (2019).

REFERENCES

Christensen, C. M. (1997). *The innovator's dilemma: When new technologies cause great firms to fail.* Boston, MA: Harvard Business School Press.

Goodman, E. P., & Powles, J. (2019). Urbanism under Google: Lessons from Sidewalk Toronto. *Fordham Law Review,* Forthcoming.

Jenik, I., & Lauer, K. (2017). *Regulatory sandboxes and financial inclusion* (Working Paper). Washington, DC: CGAP.

Lepore, J. (2014, June 23). The disruption machine: What the gospel of innovation gets wrong. *The New Yorker.*

Marcuse, H. (1968). *Negations: Essays in critical theory* (p. xxiii). London: Allen Lane.

Mazzucato, M. (2015). *The entrepreneurial state: Debunking public vs. private sector myths.* London: Anthem Press.

Vinsel, L. (2019). *Moving violations, automobiles, experts, and regulations in the United States.* Baltimore: Johns Hopkins University Press.

REFERENCES

Adam, B., & Groves, C. (2007). *Future matters: Action, knowledge, ethics.* Leiden: Brill.

Arendt, H. (1958/1998). *The human condition.* Chicago: University of Chicago Press.

Autor, D. (2019, January 4). *Work of the past, work of the future.* Richard T. Ely Lecture, AEA Annual Meeting Atlanta. https://economics.mit.edu/files/16724.

Autor, D., & Salomons, A. (2018, Spring). *Is automation labor-displacing? Productivity growth, employment, and the labor share.* BPEA Conference Draft.

Awad, E., Dsouza, S., Kim, R., Schulz, J., Henrich, J., Shariff, A., et al. (2018). The moral machine experiment. *Nature, 563*(7729), 7759.

Barbrook, R., & Cameron, A. (1996). The californian ideolgy. *Science as Culture, 6*(1), 44–72.

Bartlett, J. (2018). *The people vs tech how the internet is killing democracy (and how we save it).* London: Penguin Random House.

Beck, U. (1992). *Risk society: Towards a new modernity.* London: Sage.

Bell, A. M., Chetty, R., Jaravel, X., Petkova, N., & Van Reenen, J. (2017). *Who becomes an inventor in America? The importance of exposure to innovation* (No. w24062). National Bureau of Economic Research.

Bliss, L. (2018, September 7). *How smart should a city be? Toronto is finding out.* City Lab. https://www.citylab.com/design/2018/09/how-smart-should-a-city-be-toronto-is-finding-out/569116/.

Borup, M., Brown, N., Konrad, K., & Van Lente, H. (2006). The sociology of expectations in science and technology. *Technology Analysis & Strategic Management, 18*(3–4), 285–298.

Brand, S. (1995). *How buildings learn: What happens after they're built*. London: Penguin.

Brennan, J. S., Howard, P. N., & Kleis Nielsen, R. (2018). *An industry-led debate: How UK media cover artificial intelligence*. Reuters Institute for the Study of Journalism. https://reutersinstitute.politics.ox.ac.uk/sites/default/files/2018-12/Brennen_UK_Media_Coverage_of_AI_FINAL.pdf.

Brin, S., & Page, L. (1998). The anatomy of a large-scale hypertextual web search engine. *Computer Networks and ISDN Systems, 30*(1–7), 107–117.

Brooks, H. (1994). The relationship between science and technology. *Research Policy, 23*(5), 477–486.

Broussard, M. (2018). *Artificial unintelligence: How computers misunderstand the world*. Cambridge: MIT Press.

Brynjolfsson, E., & McAfee, A. (2014). *The second machine age: Work, progress, and prosperity in a time of brilliant technologies*. New York: W. W. Norton.

Burns, L., & Shulgan, C. (2018). *Autonomy: The quest to build the driverless car and how it will reshape our world* (p. 252). London: HarperCollins.

Carr, N. (2014). *The glass cage: Automation and us*. New York: W. W. Norton.

Christensen, C. M. (1997). *The innovator's dilemma: When new technologies cause great firms to fail*. Boston, MA: Harvard Business School Press.

Clemens, M. A., Lewis, E. G., & Postel, H. M. (2018). Immigration restrictions as active labor market policy: Evidence from the Mexican bracero exclusion. *American Economic Review, 108*(6), 1468–1487.

Coiera, E. (2018). The fate of medicine in the time of AI. *Lancet, 392*(10162), 2331–2332.

Collingridge, D. (1980). *The social control of technology*. Milton Keynes: Open University Press.

Cowan, R. (1983). *More work for mother: The ironies of household technology from the open hearth to the microwave*. New York: Basic Books.

Crawford, K. (2016, June 25). Artificial intelligence's white guy problem. *New York Times*.

Dahl, R. A. (1961). *Who governs? Power and democracy in an American city*. New Haven: Yale University Press.

David, P. A. (1991). Computer and dynamo: The modern productivity paradox in a not-too-distant mirror. In *Technology and productivity: The challenge for economic policy*. The Technology Economy Programmer (pp. 315–347). Paris, France: OECD Publishing.

Domingos, P. (2015). *The master algorithm: How the quest for the ultimate learning machine will remake our world*. New York: Basic Books.

Elish, M. C. (2019). Moral crumple zones: Cautionary tales in human-robot interaction. *Engaging Science, Technology, and Society, 5*, 40–60.

Elish, M. C., & boyd, d. (2018). Situating methods in the magic of Big Data and AI. *Communication Monographs, 85*(1), 57–80.

Ensmenger, N. (2018). The environmental history of computing. *Technology and Culture, 59*(5), S7–S33.

Eubanks, V. (2018). *Automating inequality: How high-tech tools profile, police, and punish the poor.* New York: St. Martin's Press.

Floridi, L. (2014). The fourth revolution: How the infosphere is reshaping human reality. Oxford: Oxford University Press.

Frey, C. B., & Osborne, M. A. (2017). The future of employment: How susceptible are jobs to computerisation? *Technological Forecasting and Social Change, 114,* 254–280.

Gabo, N., & Pevsner, A. (1920). The realistic manifesto. *Russian Art of the Avant-Garde Theory and Criticism, 1902*(34), 209–214.

Glouberman, S., & Zimmerman, B. (2002). *Complicated and complex systems: What would successful reform of medicare look like?* (Discussion Paper No. 8). Commission on the Future of Health Care in Canada.

Goodman, E. P., & Powles, J. (2019). Urbanism under Google: Lessons from Sidewalk Toronto. *Fordham Law Review,* Forthcoming.

Guellec, D., & Paunov, C. (2017). *Digital innovation and the distribution of income* (No. w23987). National Bureau of Economic Research.

Guston, D. H. (2014). Understanding 'anticipatory governance'. *Social Studies of Science, 44*(2), 218–242.

Halevy, A., Norvig, P., & Pereira, F. (2009). The unreasonable effectiveness of data. *IEEE Intelligent Systems, 24*(2), 8–12.

Hughes, T. P. (1993). *Networks of power: Electrification in Western society, 1880–1930.* Baltimore: Johns Hopkins University Press.

Jacobs, J. (1961). *The death and life of great American cities.* New York, NY: Vintage.

Jasanoff, S. (2016). *The ethics of invention: Technology and the human future.* New York: W. W. Norton.

Jenik, I., & Lauer, K. (2017). *Regulatory sandboxes and financial inclusion* (Working Paper). Washington, DC: CGAP.

Joy, B. (2000, April 1). Why the future doesn't need us. *Wired Magazine.* https://www.wired.com/2000/04/joy-2/.

Kelly, K. (2010). *What technology wants.* New York: Penguin.

Keynes, J. M. (1933). Economic possibilities for our grandchildren. In *Essays in persuasion.* London: Palgrave Macmillan.

Kohler, T. A., Smith, M. E., Bogaard, A., Feinman, G. M., Peterson, C. E., Betzenhauser, A., et al. (2017). Greater post-Neolithic wealth disparities in Eurasia than in North America and Mesoamerica. *Nature, 551*(7682), 619.

Lanier, J. (2011). *You are not a gadget: A manifesto.* New York: Vintage.

Lepore, J. (2014, June 23). The disruption machine: What the gospel of innovation gets wrong. *The New Yorker.*

Lessig, L. (2000, January 1). Code is law: On liberty in cyberspace. *Harvard Magazine*. https://harvardmagazine.com/2000/01/code-is-law-html.

Levin, K., Cashore, B., Bernstein, S., & Auld, G. (2012, 23 May). Overcoming the tragedy of super wicked problems: Constraining our future selves to ameliorate global climate change. *Policy Sciences, 45*(2), 123–152. https://doi.org/10.1007/s11077-012-9151-0.

MacKenzie, D. (1984). Marx and the machine. *Technology and Culture, 25*(3), 473–502.

Marcuse, H. (1968). *Negations: Essays in critical theory* (p. xxiii). London: Allen Lane.

Mateescu, A., & Elish, M. C. (2019). *AI in context: The labor of integrating new technologies*. Data & Society Research Institute. Accessed at https://apo.org.au/node/217456 on 21 March 2019.

Mazzucato, M. (2015). *The entrepreneurial state: Debunking public vs. private sector myths*. London: Anthem Press.

McCarthy, J. (1983). The little thoughts of thinking machines. *Psychology Today, 17*(12), 46–49.

McDowell-Naylor, D. (2018). *The participatory, communicative, and organisational dimensions of public-making: Public engagement and the development of autonomous vehicles in the United Kingdom* (Unpublished PhD thesis). Royal Holloway, University of London.

McGreal, C. (2018). *American overdose: The opioid tragedy in three acts*. London: Guardian Faber.

Mody, C. C. (2016). *The long arm of Moore's law: Microelectronics and American science*. Cambridge: MIT Press.

Morozov, E. (2013). *To save everything, click here: The folly of technological solutionism*. Public Affairs.

Nelson, R. R. (1977). *The moon and the ghetto: An essay on public policy analysis*. New York: W. W. Norton.

Norton, P. D. (2008). *Fighting traffic: The dawn of the motor age in the American city*. Cambridge: MIT Press.

Nowotny, H. (2010). *Insatiable curiosity: Innovation in a fragile future*. Cambridge: MIT Press.

Nye, D. E. (1994). *American technological sublime*. Cambridge: MIT Press.

Olhede, S. C., & Wolfe, P. J. (2018). The growing ubiquity of algorithms in society: Implications, impacts and innovations. *Philosophical Transactions of the Royal Society A: Mathematical, Physical and Engineering Sciences, 376*(2128), art. 20170364.

O'Neil, C. (2017). *Weapons of math destruction: How big data increases inequality and threatens democracy*. New York: Broadway Books.

Paquet, G. (2003). *Governance as subversive bricolage in the 21st century.* http://
citeseerx.ist.psu.edu/viewdoc/download?doi=10.1.1.507.2404&rep=rep1&
type=pdf.

Perez, C. (2010, June). *The advance of technology and major bubble collapses: Historical regularities and lessons for today.* Paper for the Engelsberg Seminar on 'The
Future of Capitalism', Ax:son Foundation, Sweden. http://www.carlotaperez.
org/downloads/media/PEREZTechnologyandbubblesforEngelsbergseminar.
pdf.

Piketty, T. (2014). *Capital in the twenty-first century.* Cambridge: Harvard University Press.

Pollock, N., & Williams, R. (2016). *How industry analysts shape the digital future.*
Oxford: Oxford University Press.

Prates, M. O., Avelar, P. H., & Lamb, L. (2018). *Assessing gender bias in machine
translation—A case study with Google translate.* arXiv preprint arXiv:1809.
02208.

Rittel, H. W., & Webber, M. M. (1973). Dilemmas in a general theory of planning.
Policy Sciences, 4(2), 155–169.

Rogers, E. M. (1962). *Diffusion of innovations.* New York: Simon & Schuster.

Rushkoff, D. (2016). *Throwing rocks at the Google bus: How growth became the enemy
of prosperity.* New York: Penguin.

Scannell, J. W., Blanckley, A., Boldon, H., & Warrington, B. (2012). Diagnosing
the decline in pharmaceutical R&D efficiency. *Nature Reviews Drug Discovery,
11*(3), 191.

Sclove, R. (1995). *Democracy and technology.* New York: Guilford Press.

Scott, J. C. (1998). *Seeing like a state: How certain schemes to improve the human
condition have failed.* New Haven: Yale University Press.

Seely Brown, J., & Paul D. (2000, April 13). *A response to Bill Joy and the doom-and
gloom technofuturists.* The Industry Standard. http://engl102-fl2-lombardy.
wikispaces.umb.edu/file/view/A+Response+to+Bill+Joy+and+the+Doom+
and+Gloom+Technofuturists+by+John+Seely+Brown+and+Paul+Duguid.pdf.

Smith, M. R., & Marx, L. (Eds.). (1994). *Does technology drive history? The dilemma
of technological determinism.* Cambridge: MIT Press.

Sparrow, R., & Howard, M. (2017). When human beings are like drunk robots:
Driverless vehicles, ethics, and the future of transport. *Transportation Research
Part C: Emerging Technologies, 80,* 206–215.

Stilgoe, J. (2018). Machine learning, social learning and the governance of self-
driving cars. *Social Studies of Science, 48*(1), 25–56.

Sudjic, D. (2009). *The language of things: Understanding the world of desirable
objects.* New York: W. W. Norton.

Susskind, J. (2018). *Future politics: Living together in a world transformed by tech.*
Oxford: Oxford University Press.

Swierstra, T., & Rip, A. (2007). Nano-ethics as NEST-ethics: Patterns of moral argumentation about new and emerging science and technology. *Nanoethics, 1*(1), 3–20.

Vaidhyanathan, S. (2018). *Antisocial media: How Facebook disconnects us and undermines democracy.* Oxford: Oxford University Press.

Van Lente, H. (2000). Forceful futures: From promise to requirement. In N. Brown & B. Rappert (Eds.), *Contested futures: A sociology of prospective techno-science* (pp. 43–64). London: Routledge.

Villani, C. (2018). *For a meaningful artificial intelligence: Towards a French and European strategy.* https://www.aiforhumanity.fr/pdfs/MissionVillani_Report_ENG-VF.pdf.

Vinsel, L. (2019). *Moving violations, automobiles, experts, and regulations in the United States.* Baltimore: Johns Hopkins University Press.

Walker, R. (2018). *Pictures of a gone city: Tech and the dark side of prosperity in the San Francisco Bay Area.* Oakland: PM Press.

Weinberg, A. M. (1966). Can technology replace social engineering? *Bulletin of the Atomic Scientists, 12*(10), 4–8.

Weizenbaum, J. (1976). *Computer power and human reason: From judgment to calculation.* San Francisco: W. H. Freeman.

Wetmore, J. M. (2007). Amish technology: Reinforcing values and building community. *IEEE Technology and Society Magazine, 26*(2), 10–21.

Williams, J. (2018). *Stand out of our light: Freedom and resistance in the attention economy.* Cambridge: Cambridge University Press.

Winner, L. (1977). *Autonomous technology: Technics-out-of-control as a theme in political thought.* Cambridge: MIT Press.

Winner, L. (1980). Do artifacts have politics? *Daedalus, 109,* 121–136.

Woodhouse, E., & Sarewitz, D. (2007). Science policies for reducing societal inequities. *Science and Public Policy, 34*(2), 139–150.

Young, M. (1958). *The rise of the meritocracy.* London: Pelican.

Zalasiewicz, J., Williams, M., Waters, C. N., Barnosky, A. D., Palmesino, J., Rönnskog, A. S., et al. (2017). Scale and diversity of the physical technosphere: A geological perspective. *The Anthropocene Review, 4*(1), 9–22.

Zuboff, S. (2019). *The age of surveillance capitalism: The fight for a human future at the new frontier of power.* New York: Public Affairs.

INDEX

Druck:
Customized Business Services GmbH
im Auftrag der
KNV Zeitfracht GmbH
Ein Unternehmen der Zeitfracht - Gruppe
Ferdinand-Jühlke-Str. 7
99095 Erfurt